T0131627

A FOOT IN BOTH

Worlds

A JOURNEY OF
TRANSFORMATION
AND GROWTH

Jen Barlow

BALBOA.
PRESS

A DIVISION OF HAY HOUSE

Balboa Press books may be ordered through booksellers or by contacting:

Balboa Press
A Division of Hay House
1663 Liberty Drive
Bloomington, IN 47403
www.balboapress.com
1 (877) 407-4847

Because of the dynamic nature of the Internet, any web addresses or links contained in this book may have changed since publication and may no longer be valid. The views expressed in this work are solely those of the author and do not necessarily reflect the views of the publisher, and the publisher hereby disclaims any responsibility for them.

The author of this book does not dispense medical advice or prescribe the use of any technique as a form of treatment for physical, emotional, or medical problems without the advice of a physician, either directly or indirectly. The intent of the author is only to offer information of a general nature to help you in your quest for emotional and spiritual well-being. In the event you use any of the information in this book for yourself, which is your constitutional right, the author and the publisher assume no responsibility for your actions.

Front cover photo by,
Elizabeth Ellen Photography
Front cover design by,
Primary Concepts

Print information available on the last page.

ISBN: 978-1-5043-3117-3 (sc)
ISBN: 978-1-5043-3118-0 (e)

Library of Congress Control Number: 2015905696

Balboa Press rev. date: 05/18/2015

To my family and friends

Contents

Acknowledgments

With deep gratitude and appreciation I extend my heart to the many teachers who have graced my path along this journey. Thank you to Rebecca, Kaia, Chloe, Adam, Derrick, Carol, Kate, and Grandmother Tree Herbals. I am grateful for the time allowed to learn and grow with you. For without you, there would be no story to share. Your guidance, love, and support are forever an energetic bond in my heart.

Thank you, Mother Earth, for allowing my existence to grow and allowing me to learn from you.

Thank you, guides, for your patience, support, pure love, and laughter. I am honored.

Thank you, Sherry, Beth, Craig, and Eileen for your assistance and talents on the cover of *A Foot in Both Worlds*. It is as beautiful as your spirits.

Thank you to my sister for your computer savvy and exceptional humor in bringing the pages of this book together.

To my husband and daughter for supporting me through a very rough awakening, I thank you. Life is a precious gift and one I am honored to share with both of you.

For all our ancestors, may we remember to respect and honor their contributions in life as well as in spirit.

Preface

As I sit in my chair staring out my window, the sun peers through the trees while the breeze gently blows the leaves. The sound of the wind rustling the leaves brings me a peaceful, relaxing feeling. High in the sky is the sound of a small airplane, a symbol of the relationship between my thoughts and a higher self that connects me to the truth of what I am thinking.

The stories in this book are from my personal journals, and I have struggled to understand these experiences. Why was I led in this direction? What was the significance of each experience? At times I was extremely frustrated and felt like a punching bag reeling from blows that knocked me into complete exhaustion. I would dig deep into my being to find the courage and strength to get to my feet and then face the next experience with curiosity, excitement, and fear. I cried often and swore even more. I had plunged into the abyss of emotional darkness because of the aftereffects of a tornado that tore apart a section of my town and my heart. I had hit my limit of feeling like garbage, and in those final moments of despair, the answer came.

I was guided to The Center, located in a midsized town within the hills of Massachusetts. I didn't know I was about to embark on a journey of spiritual awareness, a journey I would have never considered in this lifetime. In order to move forward, I had to let go of the past while working through my fears and uncontrolled emotions. I needed to remove expectations of what others thought and felt I should be. I needed to recognize and release my old thought patterns and behaviors, which enabled me to relearn who I was on a deeper level.

I was led to a Native American style of teaching, a way of life deeply rooted to Mother Earth. I frantically searched for books on the topics and beliefs I was being taught, but they didn't exist. The Native way is taught through oral history. I realized I held the key to the answers I was searching for in my heart. I wanted to know who I was. Slowly, over a two-year period, I began to see the beauty in all things and take notice of what nature was showing me. Flowers, with their intricate and delicate compositions, allowed me to breathe in their beauty and feel their essences. Countless varieties of birds sang their messages. Trees shared their strength. Forest creatures appeared on my doorstep and made their presence known until I listened to their messages.

I began to see the connection between all living things, and that opened my eyes to a higher level of consciousness. I became observant of people and places that expanded my vision of the world. This new consciousness showed me that what I had always thought were coincidences were actually synchronicities, and if I paid attention, the messages would reveal the answers I asked for. I felt driven by an unseen force to dig deep within the wells of my soul to seek the truth in all things. This knowledge assisted me in changing my perceptions and trusting in something larger than myself.

These stories are my journey and my struggle to reconnect with Spirit.

Winds of Change

Journal Entry 1

*I*t was Wednesday, which meant our Girl Scouts would be meeting after school at the local academy. Two of my friends and co-leaders, Violet and Amber, would meet me at three p.m. to assist in guiding the troop. A tornado watch had been issued for our area earlier in the day, but I didn't pay much attention to it. My focus was on our troop getting ready for our annual camping trip. This time we would be staying in a beautiful, upscale lodge, with indoor plumbing and heating! Some of the girls wanted the rustic outdoor experience, so with the academy's front yard as a practice area, they began to unpack the tent and stakes. Within fifteen minutes, one of the girls noticed a storm heading our way. I glanced up and saw the dark, foreboding sky, which made me feel uneasy. The clouds were rolling in quickly, and we needed to get inside.

"Let's pack up and head for the basement," I called to the girls.

Amid the moans and groans of some, the troop gathered up and moved the gear down the stairs without too much struggle. Working on their own, the girls had the tent almost completely erected in the basement when the first phone call came in.

"There's a tornado spotted in Northampton," Violet whispered into my ear. Her husband, Tony, was on the other end of the phone, relaying the message.

"That's not even close to us," I replied and went back to watching the girls assemble the tent while chatting with Amber. Her phone rang; it was her husband, Mark.

"The storm's getting worse and headed this way," she said softly, anxiously turning her head toward me. "Mark wants me to get the car home and into the garage."

If the impending storm was to be as bad as predicted, I understood why Mark wanted the car out of the elements. I stood by a table in the basement of the academy, trying to decide what to do next.

Pack up, I heard in my head.

"Let's pack up, girls." It was now four, and our meetings ran until five, but not this time. "Call your parents; they need to pick you up quickly." Panic rushed through my body.

We disassembled and packed away the tent within minutes. Most of the girls had cell phones, and those who didn't borrowed from the rest of us to contact a parent.

"What's going on?" one of the girls asked.

"No need to worry," I answered as calmly as I could. "A tornado has been spotted at the other end of the state." My attempt at being calm did not work, as I could see the fear in their eyes.

By four thirty, every scout had been picked up by a parent. Some had even been en route to get their kids early. My daughter, Akia, and Amber's daughter, Jess, ran for Amber's car. While the two of us decided what to do with our kids, the decision was made for us. They jumped out of her car, ran across the parking lot, and jumped into my car.

"I guess the girls are coming with me." I smiled, motioning my head toward the direction of my car. I felt relieved.

"I'll see you after the storm," Amber replied, walking to her car.

I walked toward my car and opened the driver's-side door. I grabbed the steering wheel to pull myself into the seat but stopped. I slowly turned and looked toward the western horizon. Hanging in the sky was a massive black storm cloud. I took a deep breath to calm my nerves; something was very wrong. I felt fear twisting my stomach. I glanced to my left, which was the south side of town. The clouds had a reddish-orange hue to them. I launched myself into the driver's seat, started the car, slammed it into drive, and sped toward home.

"Are we going to have a tornado?" Akia, my one and only child, asked, sinking into her seat.

"Maybe," I said, glancing back at her in the rear-view mirror.

I couldn't reach home fast enough; my mind was on full disaster alert. We pulled into the garage at a rapid speed and jumped out of the car, and I closed the garage door. I ran for the television, fumbling with all the remotes to get to the Weather Channel in time to see the entire state of Massachusetts covered in a red warning map. The message ticker below the map was tracking the storm. The tornado was headed east down the Mass Turnpike. My home was in the direct path.

Oh, crap, I thought. "Akia, grab what you need and get into the basement with Jess." I sped through the house, grabbing the checkbook, laptop, computer codes, and various paperwork. I found some water bottles and packed some clothes and flashlights. I found both cats and tossed them into the basement.

Grabbing my cell phone, I called my sister in Monson. "Come on, answer the phone!" I yelled into the speaker. I left a frantic message on her machine: "Get the boys into the basement; a tornado is heading for us."

I hung up and made another call to Jess's mom. "Amber, are you watching the weather? It's headed down the pike!" I yelled, pacing the floor in my family room.

"We're in the basement watching the weather. We're fine," she said calmly.

I then called my friend Grace. She had no idea about the tornado or the wrath about to be unleashed on the town. Her house was only yards from the turnpike, and her daughter was at another friend's house, also close to the Mass Pike.

"It's headed right for us!" I cried and quickly hung up.

I remembered the chickens. What was I going to do with them? I ran outside to the coop and scanned the area. There was nothing I could do. With a sinking heart, I said to the chickens, "You're on your own; be safe." While I was scrambling around, my husband, strangely enough, decided he wanted to grill pork chops.

"You're aware the tornado's headed right for us, right now!" I screeched at him, looking for last-minute provisions. He loves storms and wasn't the least bit fazed by what was happening. He even took out the video camera as he started grilling.

I yelled into the basement to check on the girls. They were hiding under the stairs and were panicky. I stood there alone in the family room, staring at the walls. Everything we owned had a memory attached to it. Which memories were most important to save? How could I choose? I suddenly realized I had no control over the situation, and that scared me.

An eerie silence engulfed the land. Clouds moved rapidly toward the house. The air shifted, and then the silence exploded with the sound of hail slamming the house.

Although still calm, my husband ran for the porch to grab his video camera.

"Hail always comes before the brunt of the storm!" I yelled through the screen door from the family room.

"This is cool," he commented, videotaping the storm.

The wind picked up, and the windows were shaking from the deafening force of the ice-cold hail relentlessly pelting the glass. Five minutes later, nothing.

"Is that it?" I asked him, looking toward the sky.

"I don't know," he replied, going to check on the grill.

The girls made their way up to the family room. Jess grabbed a cup from the kitchen cabinet and headed outside to pick up the huge hailstones lying on the ground.

"Where's the rest of the storm?" I was confused, as the radar showed it was heading right for us. I decided I wasn't going to take my eyes or ears off the sky. As I anxiously scanned the sky, my cell phone rang. I was not prepared for what I heard next.

"How's Jess? How's Jess?" Amber was frantic on the other end of the phone.

"She's fine; we had hail. What about you?" I asked, looking calmly out the back door.

"It's gone, it's all gone!" She was screaming.

"What are you talking about?" But I realized at that moment that the tornado had not been on our side of town. Instead, it had ripped through the south side of town, where she lived.

My husband must have heard my distress. "What's going on?" He looked concerned.

"You talk to her! I can't!" Overwhelmed, I threw the phone to him. Tears welled up in my eyes. I sat on the coffee table, and Jess stood beside me. I had known this child since she was five. Now I had to explain to her at twelve that her life had been altered in a matter of seconds. I rubbed the back of her hair.

I spoke softly. "Your house is gone, but everyone is alive and okay." There were no other words I could form at that moment. That was the hardest message I'd ever had to convey to a child.

I went to the house phone. I called my friends Grace and Ginger to tell them what happened. Both of their families immediately came to our home. My husband, John, and Ginger's husband, Matt, grabbed their chainsaws, threw them into John's truck, and drove straight into the destruction.

I anxiously dialed my sister's number; she answered quickly. The storm missed her house and they were safe. The anxiety dropped out of my body. Now I could concentrate on Amber. What was the extent of the damage? How were we going to get them out?

We all piled into my car and headed across town to Amber's home.

The bottom of her street had disappeared under the massive pine trees torn from their roots and slammed onto the road. Power lines were hidden beneath the debris, making passage impossible. We found John and Matt and contemplated our next move. The only safe option was to go back to my house and wait.

We arrived home and clicked on the Weather Channel. Another tornado was headed our way. Grace decided it was time to leave and get her kids home while Ginger and her family decided to stay. The kids scurried to the basement to make a fort under the basement stairs.

Jake and Jackie, our cats, had escaped the confines of the basement. I bent over to pick up Jake. As I flung the chubby cat over my shoulder, I glanced out the family room window. A blast of wind ripped through our backyard, bending trees with hurricane force. The wind erupted toward the house. I froze. I had seen this same vision in a dream eight years ago, and now the dream was unfolding before my eyes. I knew this couldn't be good.

"We need to get into the basement now," I said to Ginger.

We quickly moved from the family room to the basement stairs. I slammed the door as we made our way down the cellar stairs to the children and husbands who were watching the weather on the TV set in the basement. My adrenaline pulsed through my body as I paced the basement floor. My head swirled with thoughts about what that vision meant and how bad this was truly going to be. All we could do was watch, listen, and wait.

Time moved so slowly; the anticipation of what was going on outside gnawed at my gut.

After what seemed like an eternity, John walked up the basement stairs to the door leading into the family room and slowly opened it.

"It's okay, you can all come up," he said calmly.

We gathered the kids and made our way up the stairs. When I reached the top step, I stopped and glanced around the room. Everything was intact. Then, making my way to the back door, I noticed our outdoor clock had been blown over and was broken, and a few chairs had flipped over. The trees and especially the chickens were all okay. I felt huge relief as the tension momentarily dropped from my shoulders.

Within minutes of our surfacing from the basement, our house phone and cell phones started ringing. Amber's mother, who lived out of state, had tracked down our home phone number and called. I could hear and feel the sheer panic in her voice. I gave her what little information I had of the situation.

"Please get them out," she fearfully pleaded.

"I will do my best." The pressure built in my heart. I hoped I could aid in her request.

I was desperately trying to contact Amber. The only phone they had working, and with very little charge available, was her son's. We finally connected, and she thought it best to conserve what little charge was left on the phone. All we could do now was sit and wait for their call.

The phone rang at seven p.m. Our friends Amber and Mark and their son had made their long journey through the woods, climbing over trees and debris to the local school-bus company. John and Jess went to pick them up. I will never forget how they looked when they walked through the door. Muddy, bloody, and soaked from rain. That vision is burned into my memory.

That was June 1, 2011. The tornado had traveled thirty-nine miles that day. Many friends and town residents were left homeless and traumatized. Many animals were swept away or impaled. My life changed forever in the blink of an eye. The tornado didn't hit me directly in the material sense; it hit me in the emotional sense. My heart.

Our house soon became the hub of activity. Amber and Mark, their two children, two dogs, and eight chickens moved in with us. We had the space, and opening our home was the right thing to do. Their house had been torn from its foundation, and they needed a place to stay.

Calls flooded our home and cell phones for assistance. Family, friends, neighbors, schoolteachers, churches, and community centers all pitched in to help one another. People from other towns and states came. The National Guard, electric companies, and the Red Cross all came. The towns of Monson, Hampden, Wilbraham, Holland, Brimfield, Sturbridge, and numerous others across the state came together to lend a hand or heart.

It has been said that a picture is worth a thousand words. In this case, pictures could not convey the force of Mother Nature. Pine permeated the air. Trees had spun around and twisted on themselves. I sat in the uprooted tree holes for shade after many hours of climbing pile upon pile of trees while looking for anything salvageable. Glass, wood, roofing, metal, and even appliances had been carried to the hillside.

One day, armed with collection bags, some friends and I were on a quest to recover whatever we could from the debris-laden landscape. I ventured off by myself. I climbed a pile of trees, gingerly stepping from branch to branch until I found a clear spot. I carefully sat, removing the bag from across my chest, and placed it next to me. I gazed out over the now treeless horizon. I noticed the beauty that had been covered up by the forest before the tornado. I saw the steeple of the church that had been built in 1721, during the time when Ben Franklin and Blackbeard the pirate had walked on the earth.

I also saw the path of destruction. I thought, *Which do I prefer? To see the destruction or the beauty within it?* I chose to look at the beautiful hillside. As I sat there, I still couldn't comprehend why this destruction had taken place. There had to be some reason, and it eluded all my faculties at this time.

As the days and weeks progressed, the bombardment of phone calls to our home, working on cleanup, taking care of Akai and Jess, daily transporting their dogs to friends, and the integration of two different lifestyles living under one roof became stressful for all of us. I also felt an overwhelming amount of guilt that our home was left standing and theirs was taken away.

The emotional overload had become too unbearable for me. I couldn't handle everyone else's emotions anymore. I became agitated. I had no way to release my emotions, so I kept them all in. My emotions were getting more unsteady—they were up and down and frantic. I desperately looked for help through therapy. I asked friends for therapy recommendations, and called many places, only to be told there was a waiting list. Great. When I needed help the most I couldn't find it.

I sat alone at the kitchen counter and said to the air, "Please help me find someone to talk to."

My luck changed immediately. A friend recommended a therapy group about half an hour from my home. They could take me right away. I questioned my sanity all the way to the appointment.

The therapist assigned to me that day was very kind and had a quick wit and a great sense of humor. As I began to talk about the tornado and the emotional toll it took on me, everything came pouring out. I felt the emotions leaving with the words.

She explained that because of the tornado, some people were going through similar situations and it was a normal reaction. She also explained that I didn't need to return to therapy unless I wanted to. I felt free and light when I left her.

During this time, Amber had received an offer from a friend in town to live at their home while the friend was away for the summer. They accepted the offer, and we helped them move in. As summer rolled on, a trailer was brought to their property, and they moved back to their land. Amber and I resumed our morning walks, and she gave me tours of the house during different construction phases. I enjoyed seeing the rebuilding and visiting with the builder, as he was a friend of both of ours. The construction of their new house was moving quickly.

Even through these times of great movement on the building, Amber and I grew further apart. There were many times I wanted to walk away from our friendship. Emotionally I was drained. I gave every ounce of energy I had, and I had nothing left to give to anyone. Once they were in their new home, I felt that whatever I had to complete with Amber was finished. I knew our lives would spiral back around at some point in the future, but where and when was up in the air for now.

I was compelled to move onto another cause because of a brief meeting with one of Amber's neighbors. A casino had come into our town, and I felt my time and attention would be best utilized focusing on preserving the land. I called a friend who was part of this group and joined in with their efforts. The casino eventually moved out of town.

The tornado was the catalyst of my journey. The vision I'd had of the tornado eight years before it blew into my life was my wakeup call to start living my life the way it was meant to be lived. What did that truly mean? To live my life the way it was meant to be lived? What was the purpose of the tornado, and how did it fit into my life's work?

The answers would slowly be revealed.

Seeking the Truth

Journal Entry 2

Every year around February or March, I would get a feeling I was forgetting to do something yet couldn't remember what it was I needed to do. So one day I turned on the computer and waited for it to boot up. Where to begin my search? There was an endless amount of cyber information, so I narrowed the search by typing in Massachusetts ghost hunters and paranormal groups. My gut didn't feel right with those choices, so I typed intuition, and that felt right.

The Center popped up and caught my attention. I noticed a survey and took it. I found I answered yes to many questions, such as I get premonitions, I get unexplained moods, and I answer people's sentences before they finish speaking. Then I ran across their e-mail address and debated endlessly in my head about contacting them for more information. I mustered up enough nerve and sent an e-mail request.

The response to the e-mail came very quickly from a woman named Kate. She was happy to speak with me, and we set a mutually agreed-upon date and time to meet. I was extremely nervous. What was I going to talk about, and why was I even going there? I kept my appointment quiet from my family because I didn't know what I was being called there for, let alone try to explain the calling to them.

I printed the directions off the Internet, laid them safely down on the passenger seat next to me, and set off on my journey. The trip was going well until the directions led me further away from the area I needed to be in. I decided to do what I always did when I got turned around when driving: I felt for the pull in my chest.

"I know that feeling," I said to myself.

I use the feeling all the time when I drive; I call it my internal GPS. I decided to follow it. The pull led me to a very narrow driveway with a steep incline. Waiting outside were two adorable dogs wagging their tails and barking happily. A tall woman with long dark hair and what looked like a Native American-style bag around her neck approached the car. I wondered what I had gotten myself into. She reached out to hug me as she welcomed me. This made me feel uneasy. I didn't like to hug people and never understood why, but I felt it polite to do so in this case.

We climbed the back steps to the porch. The property was covered in an abundance of tall pine trees. As I entered through the side door of the house, I had an overwhelming feeling of calmness and peace. We walked down the hallway to the kitchen, and as we took our seats at the kitchen table, we began to talk. I felt comfortable in the space, and my experiences began to flow from my lips.

Kate was one of the calmest people I had ever met. She never judged me or hinted in any way with her body language that I was crazy as I tried to explain the unexplainable. I was the one questioning my own sanity. We talked for two hours, and time seemed to stand still. I was absorbing everything she was explaining to me and wanted more knowledge. I was curious about why premonitions would be shown to me and what the meanings behind the numerous visions meant, especially the tornado.

Kate asked if I had ever grounded myself. I had no idea what she was talking about. She asked for permission to touch my shoulders and I agreed. I am not usually comfortable with a stranger touching me, but I felt comfortable with her.

As soon as she touched my shoulders, I had a vision of a wide-open field of wildflowers. Bright and healthy flowers swayed back and forth from an unseen breeze. An extremely intense white light warmed me from the inside out. It was the most beautiful place I had ever seen. Then it was gone. I didn't want it to go away; I wanted to see more. This vision was spectacular, yet I did not understand the significance or meaning of it. Did this aid me in being grounded? What does being grounded even mean? I felt good inside, but none of this made any sense.

I felt safe to share an experience I had in my dream state. About ten years ago, two small children disappeared from their home in the Midwest. During the dream, I saw a boy and a girl in a dark, wet hole. Above them was a sewer pipe dripping water. The girl had already passed on, and the boy was on his way. I shot straight up in bed with sweat dripping from my head, my heart pounding.

The next day my sister called me. She had been watching the news and explained how two children were found dead in the Midwest in a sewer. My heart sank, and I felt overwhelmingly sad and sick to my stomach. The dream I'd had became reality, and I was deeply bothered by it. Why did I see this? Could I have prevented it? I asked Kate these questions. She explained the children had come to me for help in crossing over. I just sat there and stared at her with my eyebrows raised in disbelief. How could that be possible? It was a dream that just happened to be a coincidence—wasn't it?

Kate explained that The Center ran classes to understand the things I had answered on the survey as well as things in my dreams. Maybe this was the feeling I was getting year after year, to come here to get answers to the visions and premonitions that caught my attention time and time again.

I decided to attend a class with my friend Ginger to see if it would be of value. We booked a session with Derrick, who would be teaching the class. The session was an hour long, and we worked on some basic techniques. I was intrigued and decided that night that I would take the class. Ginger was also intrigued, but the class was not for her. I wondered if the vision of the tornado was connected to this class in some way. I guess I would have to wait and see, and patience was not one of my virtues.

Class of Energy

Journal Entry 3

Growing up, I watched everything available on TV, which wasn't much because we didn't have cable or instant movies in the 1970's. Our family owned one TV set, which the entire family had to share. There were no remote controls to fight over, which meant we actually had to get up from our comfy chairs and change the channels by hand. Most of the time the reception was poor, and we used a tuner, a set of wires resting on top of the oversized TV. Turning the dial on the tuner somehow tuned the TV until we clearly saw a picture.

I have always been fascinated by ghosts. I wondered what it would be like to encounter a spirit. *The Night Stalker*, *Project Bluebook*, even *Star Trek* drew me into the mysteries of the universe. As I grew older, technology grew, and reality shows about paranormal activities increased. The showing of haunted destinations and historic sites with haunted battlefields intrigued me. I couldn't get enough. The more I thirsted for explanations, the more baffled I became. There never seemed to be solutions or concrete answers as to why these phenomena happened. I wanted the truth.

Derrick, my teacher, knew how fascinated I was with spirits. When I arrived at class one evening, he asked if I would like to do a ghost investigation on the property. I didn't hesitate, although I was nervous.

"Try it," he said, handing me the camera.

We headed toward the side porch and walked down the stone stairway. As we rounded the corner, we saw Kate sitting on the front steps talking with a friend. We explained the adventure we were about to embark on.

"Just call to them," she said calmly.

My brain decided to get in the way. Thoughts streamed through my consciousness: How was I going to contact a spirit? I thought back to all the books I had read on intentions. Thoughts follow intentions; therefore, I had to have the purity of the intent as well. Did I have enough faith, and was I worthy to contact a spirit? I decided to give it a try.

I grounded myself, which connects ones energy with the Earth's energy to balance and center oneself, cleared my mind, stated my intention, and waited. Within seconds I felt a pull in the middle of my stomach and scanned the area with my own energy. It's the same internal GPS feeling I'd used to find my way to The Center, and it worked on this experience as well. I found that interesting.

Two large pine trees stood thirty feet in front of me. I raised the camera to my eyes, took a deep breath, and pressed the button. I couldn't believe what I was seeing: two balls of energy on the screen. Then the doubt set in.

You need a comparison, I thought.

I walked a few feet to the right side of the yard where the space felt empty and stared into the dark woods. Raising the camera into the darkness, I snapped a picture. The screen was dark; I had the answer I'd set out to find. The pull I felt on the other side of the yard was energy, spirit energy. I showed Derrick the images captured on the screen.

"We tried this with our class, but we didn't get anything." he said while looking at the screen and smiling.

We walked up the back steps, opened the sliding glass door, and stepped inside to finish the class for the evening. Although not completely convinced of my first attempt at ghost investigations, I sent the picture to a friend. She had invited me over one evening to show me her findings. Brightly colored energy fields surrounded both of the energy balls. I was beginning to see connections to energy, but I didn't understand my relationship to it.

A New Student

$\mathcal{M}$eeting new people at the center for class was always fun and exciting. Students came and went through a rotating door, until one day the door stopped rotating. For three months the door stayed closed, and then the universe opened it. A new student was about to walk through and alter my life. I wondered who this new person was when a vision of a young woman with long dark hair and glasses quickly entered my stream of consciousness.

An excited nervousness gnawed at my stomach as I pulled into the driveway. Was my vision really of the person waiting inside tonight?

I stepped out of the car and took a deep breath; there was no turning back now. I climbed the steps toward the back porch and walked inside. The new student was exactly the girl I had seen in my vision, and now she was in front of me. Chloe had entered the next phase of my life.

Class was even more amazing now that Chloe had entered my life, and I loved the excitement of learning the spiritual world with her and Derrick. I couldn't wait once a week for class because I was now an active participant living out my quest for knowledge. During class time, we did exercises that were logically impossible and intuitively accurate, yet I would experience sensations I could not understand.

The answers, I thought, had to be written down somewhere. I downloaded every book imaginable onto my Amazon Kindle phone app. I read and reread the material. Every book had the same general idea nicely wrapped in the author's own experiences, yet no concrete answers, which severely frustrated me. I was determined to find what I was in search of, although I had no idea what that truly was. Chloe held a key to a lot of the information that would slowly become unlocked within me. She knew on a deep level what I could do, though I was clueless.

One night after class I asked Chloe if she would like to carpool, and she agreed. Every week I picked her up, and this would give us time before and after class to chat. On one particular evening, Chloe seemed different. It felt as though she had something to say but did not know how.

"I think we should hang out more," she suggested from the passenger seat of the SUV.

"I was thinking the same thing," I said nervously. "I've got to tell you I'm not that great with boundaries. I am usually an all or nothing kind of friend."

Chloe started jumping up and down in her seat. "So am I!" she said, laughing excitedly.

The decision had been made. A new friendship and journey was about to unfold.

During this time, Chloe asked if I would go on a field trip with her to look at banquet halls for a future endeavor and I agreed. She arrived early one morning at my home, and we began a journey that took us deep into the countryside. We talked and laughed as we wound our way through the backwoods of a very picturesque town.

We reached our destination, which was a beautiful reproduction of a colonial home. I have always been drawn to historical homes and sites, and this place felt natural to me. The co-owner and chef took us on a tour of the facilities. We were led to the guest accommodations and the honeymoon suite, which were elegantly simple, light, and airy.

As we headed toward the very last room and stepped over the threshold, the room began to feel heavy and uninviting. I quickly turned around and headed out the door because the feeling made me very uncomfortable. Chloe was not too far behind me. We thanked the owner for the tour and returned to Chloe's car.

"I really liked that last room," Chloe said, adjusting herself in the driver's seat.

"That's the room that gave me the creeps and made me feel heavy," I remarked, clenching my fist toward the middle of my chest.

"That's what a spirit presence feels like to you," she remarked, backing out of the driveway like this was an everyday occurrence for her.

As we meandered our way through the farmlands, the GPS stopped functioning. We decided to use our own internal guidance systems to find our way.

Along the way, we chatted about life when a thought raced across my mind. "I feel like you're supposed to open my third eye, and I'm supposed to center and balance you," I jokingly said, waving my arms in the air.

Chloe slammed her hands down on the top of the steering wheel; she turned her big brown eyes toward me and stared. "It's about time!" she said with a sigh of relief.

I had no idea what she was talking about.

"It only took you three months; I almost walked away from you." She giggled. "I've been waiting for you to realize this."

The light bulb turned on; we were meant to work together on a deep level.

As our friendship progressed, Chloe was having more and more spirit issues in her apartment. A little spirit girl had been trying to get her attention, and Chloe was not willing to acknowledge her. I was not sure why she was ignoring the little girl.

One night as I pulled into her driveway to pick her up for class, I decided to see if I could feel the spirit girl's energy and immediately did.

As Chloe approached the car, I lost the connection.

"Hey, you do have a spirit girl here." I smiled as she climbed into my vehicle.

"I thought so. Where?" she asked, looking as if she already knew.

"Over there," I replied, nodding my head toward a stump.

We headed to class, and upon our arrival we shared our story with Derrick. Chloe was explaining how persistent the spirit girl was becoming.

"We need to do something," I said to Derrick.

"I'll talk with Kate and see what she says." He smiled, and we proceeded with our lesson.

A few classes went by, and I didn't understand what was taking so long to get Chloe assistance with the spirit girl. I asked Derrick what was happening, and he explained we didn't have to go to Chloe's place; we could contact her while in class.

How was that possible? I was absolutely dumbfounded.

Be Careful What You Ask For!

Journal Entry 5

The spirit girl was determined to get Chloe's attention, but Chloe wasn't ready to acknowledge her. While typing on her computer one afternoon, Chloe quickly glanced toward a tissue box on the table next to her. An unseen force slowly pushed a tissue back inside the box. Chloe knew it was the spirit, and that scared her.

When I picked Chloe up for class that night, our conversation revolved around what happened that afternoon. We decided to speak with Derrick as soon as we arrived at the center.

"We need to do something; Chloe is having increased spirit issues," I said impatiently.

"We can contact her from here," he answered, looking at us.

I had an overwhelming feeling that Chloe was uncomfortable with what we were about to do. However, I was extremely excited to do this and decided to ignore my feelings about Chloe.

Derrick walked toward the bookcase next to Chloe. Gently removing a red candle from the bookcase, he placed it in the center of the table. He picked up a book of matches lying on a small table near the kitchen. He then flipped the light switch off and the room became dark. Striking the match against the box, he lit the wick.

"Let's hold hands and say a protection prayer," he said, reaching for our hands.

We extended our hands and placed them in his; we sat in silence.

"We invite the child who is connected to Chloe to please join us," Derrick said calmly and respectfully.

Chloe began to fidget in her chair. I felt a slow cold breeze waft over my hands, which were resting on the table.

"Do you feel that?" I asked excitedly. I rose from my seat and followed the breeze into the kitchen. Feeling the flow of air, I raised my hands.

"There's the source." The kitchen window was open and a breeze was meandering through. I giggled. "Debunked." I leaned over the sink and closed the window.

While we waited for something to happen we chatted.

Chloe's eyes suddenly darted across the room to the front hall.

"Over there—something just popped its head up; something is peeking over the wall." She stared intently at the wall.

I couldn't see anything.

"There's another one." She pointed to the wall. "There are two watching us."

I felt the energy around me. "There is a lot of activity in here," I said, sensing the environment. The best way I can describe sensing or feeling the energy around me is by paying attention to how my body feels before, during, and after a particular experience. There is a shift in the energy around me that could be a very heavy feeling or a very light and airy feeling. Because of these numerous energetic experiences, I have become aware of how I am affected by energy.

In the middle of all this activity, one of the dogs who resides at The Center brought a braided rope chew to me. I reached down to pick it up.

"Hey, guys, do you feel that?" My left hand felt as though it was plunged into ice water.

I sat up. The dog abruptly stopped playing with the rope and intently watched the air. The temperature in the room changed rapidly. An ice-cold breeze rolled across my lap. I glanced over at Chloe. Her eyes were wide, and she looked frozen. I had seen that look on her face once before in class, and that was when a spirit had manifested its torso outside the sliding-glass door.

"What?" I asked, trying to remain calm.

She didn't answer.

"What do you see?" I took a deep breath. "What do you see?"

Chloe looked above my head.

"He's behind you." She was frightened.

I thought, *Oh, crap, who's behind me? The one with the icy-cold presence? Be calm, loving, and respectful* raced through my head.

Then out it came. "Please join us." *Why did I just say that?*

The cold breeze moved over my entire body.

"Derrick, Chloe, look at this," I said, pulling the sleeve of my shirt up until it could go no further.

My arm was covered in goose bumps; the temperature was bone-chilling. Imagine one of those ice-cold wintry days when the temperature plummets and it's so cold you can't get warm no matter what you do. That's how I felt: cold inside out.

I glanced at Chloe. "It's moving toward you."

"I feel it," she said hesitantly.

The presence had drifted over me, or maybe even through me, and headed toward Chloe, who was sitting to my right. She looked scared as she watched the spirit move into the gathering room.

Within minutes the temperature of the room rose. The warmth was returning to The Center. The Spirit was gone. We sat in silence, wondering who we just had contact with. Chloe looked totally spooked. Derrick grabbed the white sage and began to smudge the room. When he finished, he looked at the two of us.

"I need to ground you two," he said, pointing to the healing table.

We agreed. My physical body was shivering, and I just wanted to get warm again.

Looking back on this experience, I can understand that I had gained some knowledge. Contacting spirits was much easier than I thought. In fact, it was very easy to unknowingly open a door for all spirits to pass through. Because we were taught to be in a place of love and respect, we were able to handle ourselves and stay safe throughout this experience.

As I sit and reflect on this chapter almost a year later, I feel it necessary to expand on what I have learned. Energy is extremely powerful, moves with lightning speed, and can severely hurt you without your having knowledge or the wisdom to handle what you may encounter. I do not suggest looking for anything on your own. Let your intuition guide you when seeking a mentor or teacher. If your intuition or gut instinct doesn't feel right, honor that feeling, always!

After Life

Journal Entry 6

My life has been an ongoing quest to answer, "Why am I here?" Ghost hunting was the connection to this question. The spirit world intrigued me, and I felt there were so many missing answers. Shows about paranormal mysteries fed my desire and thrill of the unknown, yet the shows always left a void. Why were there never any concrete answers? My next class would fill a portion of the void.

Derrick decided to take a vacation, and that meant Kate would fill in as our teacher for the evening. Chloe and I were apprehensive about class because we knew Kate didn't joke around as much as we did with Derrick.

We walked through the door and quickly took our seats like nervous schoolchildren on the first day of class. To our surprise, Kate was very patient and funny.

"I spoke with Derrick about your last class," she said, looking at Chloe.

"That was an amazing class," I gleefully interjected.

"It was dangerous. This house is well-protected and you got lucky," she said in a caring, motherly tone.

I didn't understand what she meant.

"Imagine throwing a party. You invite friends, and those friends invite friends until the party gets out of hand. You have no idea who is at your party and if they are ever going to leave. You never invite something in."

We sat in silence and my brain went numb.

"You can call her," Kate softly said, intently watching Chloe.

I felt a private conversation was taking place in my presence and thought it wise to keep quiet.

Kate rose from her seat and walked behind Chloe, placing her hands on Chloe's shoulders. Within minutes, Chloe jerked forward in her seat, almost falling to the floor. Kate steadied her and then walked back to her seat. I felt dizzy and light from the energy swirling around me. *What just happened?* I thought, sitting there speechless.

When Chloe pulled herself together, she explained that the spirit girl had gone into the "white light," where others waited to receive her. My mind was whirling, trying to put a logical connection to the experience. The reality of my conscious physical world was unraveling.

My mind wandered, and I remembered a story my mother shared with me about my great-grandmother, who passed away when I was eleven. At the time, she had an experience in which she went into the "white light" and was told this too would pass. These two experiences clicked in my head that an afterlife did indeed exist.

I drove home in complete silence. I was speechless and in shock. The experience had a profound effect on me; Spirits and the afterlife existed.

Without realizing it, I had made my way home. I quietly tiptoed into my daughter's bedroom and kissed her on the check good night. I made my way upstairs to bed, where my husband was already asleep, and laid down next to him. I pulled the covers over my head and closed my eyes, glad this day was over. The world I had perceived shifted my consciousness into a higher awareness. This shift triggered fear and doubt about everything I had been taught throughout my lifetime. I needed more knowledge to figure out what was happening to me.

The next class was going to be a complete bend of my mind.

Lessons to Learn

Journal Entry 7

One evening during class, my turn came to practice energy work on Chloe. Energy work, or energy healing, is the movement of energy along points within the body. I had practiced many times on other people, and I was excited to work on Chloe. I asked Derrick to help ground me before the session, which gave me a feeling of security. I stepped to the table where Chloe was lying down and placed my hands on her.

"Ouch, you're hurting me!" Chloe snapped.

I quickly removed my hands. An adrenalin rush of fear shot through my body. What just happened? Why was she in pain? I had no clue what was happening. A thought raced through my mind that said, *That's it; I'm finished doing energy work for the night.*

"Okay, let's try this again," Derrick continued with optimism.

A wave of panic engulfed me. I was extremely hesitant to continue. My emotions were swirling with anxiety, my mind racing with confusion. Taking many deep breaths, I grounded myself again and walked to the table. My eyes locked with Chloe's.

"Do it right." She was serious, which rarely happened with us.

Do what right? I thought I *was* doing the session right. I had done many others sessions with success and this was the first time it was going all wrong.

"Come on; be nice," Derrick jabbed at Chloe.

Nervously, I began again. With each step I was unsure and anxious, hoping it would all be over soon. When finished, I slowly stepped away from the table and sat down.

"I don't feel well; I'm really cold." Chloe was struggling to push herself up with her elbows.

I began to panic inside.

Chloe slid off the table and placed her feet on the floor. Making her way to the radiator, she pulled the hood of her sweatshirt around her face and rocked back and forth. She was shivering. "I don't know what's wrong with me."

Derrick seemed unsure of what to do. "I don't know what to tell you."

Chloe wanted to call Kate, who coincidently was at The Center that evening.

Derrick seemed hesitant to contact Kate. "I don't know if we should call her for this."

I leaned forward toward Chloe and said, "Call Kate." I knew Chloe should not leave The Center feeling this way.

Chloe made her way to the kitchen table: she grabbed her cell phone and dialed the number. She asked Kate to come down here. She hung up and went back to the radiator.

Kate came downstairs and knew instantly what was wrong. Chloe climbed back onto the table, and Kate sorted out the situation.

"I just don't understand you!" Kate's words hit me straight in the heart, and it took all I had to hold back the tears.

I watched my friend lying on the table and knew I could have severely hurt her. I was scared and didn't understand what went wrong with the energy healing process.

We all sat in silence for a moment. Kate leaned forward in her chair. "What have you all learned from this experience?"

Chloe was the first to answer. "I should have listened to my own intuition."

I feel Chloe may have wanted to stop the session, like I did.

Kate said to Derrick, "You need to listen."

Kate turned her head toward me. "And you?" She waited for my answer.

I could barely answer. "I should have listened to my intuition and stopped the session."

When Chloe felt better, we made our way to the car.

"I don't hate you." It was as if she was reading my thoughts.

I appreciated the words but couldn't forgive myself.

My mind was endlessly looping the session in my head. What went on with the three of us that night? Why did the incident happen? For the life of me, I couldn't figure out the reasons. A tough decision had to be made about continuing with my training, and I decided I never wanted to do energy work again. I did, however, want to continue taking classes.

One afternoon while cleaning the house, a quick vision passed through my mind. I saw Chloe in my spare bedroom upstairs. I knew at that moment I was being given a message to get ready for a temporary houseguest. I was curious about when this vision would become reality and was again frustrated with learning patience. I would just have to sleep on the information, and that's what I did.

Waking from a restless night's sleep, I had the distinct feeling Chloe had been trying to contact me. Rolling to my left, I grabbed my cell phone from the nightstand. I turned it on with one eye open and became temporarily blinded by the intense light. Fumbling to find the text button, I pushed it.

I felt her stress through the message. "Please answer me."

I made my way to the kitchen to avoid waking my husband and called Chloe.

This can't be good, I thought, rubbing my eyes. "What's going on?" I asked nervously.

"I'm safe, but I need a place to stay tonight," Chloe whispered anxiously. She was on her way to an appointment and assured me she would call when she was finished.

I hung up, left the phone on the kitchen counter, got dressed, and went outside to do yard work. When I came back a few hours later to check my phone, there were numerous texts from her. I called her back immediately.

"I'm packing," she whispered.

"I'll check with my family and call you back," I said, feeling uneasy. Now I understood the vision.

I was beginning to see that receiving the visions was the easy part. Conveying the messages was a bit more difficult to those who had never experienced this type of communication or even believed it existed. I often found myself in this type of situation.

I called a brief family meeting to explain some of the details of the situation. Chloe and her fiancé were having difficulties in their relationship and she needed a temporary place to stay. My husband was hesitant because of the stress the tornado experience had put on our family. I explained this was a totally different circumstance and that Chloe would not be here long. He hesitantly agreed to two weeks only. My daughter had the final vote and would only agree if there was no talk of anything spiritual in the house. I accepted her wishes and called Chloe back.

"Okay, you can come here," I said, relieved that she had someplace to go.

I was on pins and needles waiting for her to arrive because I had no idea what she was experiencing at her place. She finally arrived around dinner time. I showed her to the upstairs bedroom and left her to her thoughts. A while later she came downstairs to the kitchen.

"I need to talk to you," she said as we walked to the front hallway together.

"What's going on?"

"I can't stay here yet. You know what you have to do," she said, fidgeting.

"I understand." I really didn't want to do what she was nonverbally suggesting.

I needed to contact Kate about the energy healing gone wrong, and that was not appealing to me. I did not know why Chloe had to leave my house at that moment.

Chloe headed upstairs to grab her bags. On her way out of the house, she said good-bye to my family as I followed her down the back stairs to her car.

"Where will you go?" I asked apprehensively.

"I've slept in my car before. I'll be all right." She smiled.

That didn't make me feel any better. "Call me when you get to wherever you're going," I said with trepidation.

We hugged good-bye and she drove off. I spent the evening worried. I couldn't take the stress in my head anymore, so I texted her. She was all right and safe. I was relieved.

I was terrified to contact Kate about my future at The Center. Gathering up enough nerve, I sent an e-mail requesting a meeting.

When the day came for our meeting, the anxiety swelled within me; I was shaking inside. Arriving at The Center intensified the feeling and I could not control my emotions. I went inside and sat at the kitchen table.

"Well," she said.

As I spoke, the tears streamed out of my eyes. "I want to stay in class."

She got up and got me some tissues. I hated to cry in private, never mind in front of anyone.

"You are immature and irresponsible." Her words slammed down like a hammer on my shoulders. "We do not just do things when doing spiritual work." Her words cut deeper into my heart.

I wish I knew what she meant. I was struggling to understand what spiritual work actually was.

"Do you want to continue with class?" she asked.

"Yes." My head hung low.

"Okay then."

The meeting was over. I stood to leave, and she gave me a hug.

"You have courage," she said, watching me leave.

It sure didn't feel like courage. I left The Center wrung out, weak, and emotionally drained. I spiraled into a confused state and nothing made sense. How could I be immature and irresponsible and courageous at the same time?

Reflecting on this class, I now can see a couple of areas I was blinded to. The first was paying attention and listening to my own intuition. Even though the concept of spiritual work was completely overwhelming and confusing to me, my heart always held the answers, if I could get past myself. Learning to quiet my mind enough to listen to my heart was extremely difficult. My mind was constantly thinking about everything that went wrong during the session and why it went wrong. It got to the point where I couldn't hear my own intuition anymore. I was in a complete state of bewilderment and couldn't seem to break free from it.

I thought, *Does my purpose actually involve healing energy?*

I was going to have to wait for the answer to reveal itself once again.

Reiki

Journal Entry 8

I was beating myself up relentlessly for hurting Chloe and couldn't let it go. One day the idea of taking a reiki class streamed through my consciousness. The local community center was offering the class, and I decided to register. I needed to know if I could work on another human being again. I asked Chloe if she would take the class with me, and she agreed. A few days later, she called to tell me her mother and a friend would be joining us from out of state.

The day of the class came and I felt I should leave home early, which turned out to be beneficial because Chloe's mom, Victoria, and her friend Emily pulled into the parking lot right after I arrived. We exchanged pleasantries and then gathered our bags and proceeded inside the building. Walking up the creaky old stairs, we made our way to the instructor and introduced ourselves. We placed our bags on a table and then mingled with other students until Chloe arrived. Soon after her arrival, an old friend I hadn't seen in about a year walked through the door. We hugged one another and caught up on each other's lives. It was so good to see her again, and I knew our reconnection was important. Soon the whole class arrived and we began.

The first exercise required each of us to pull a tarot card from the instructor's deck. When my turn came, I slid my hand across the top of the deck and reached for a card.

Chloe grabbed my hand, stopping me in mid-reach. "That's not your card; scan again."

I scanned the entire deck again, watching her eyes as if looking for a clue.

"That's your card." She nodded, as if to say pick it up.

I picked up the card. I flipped it, quickly wondering what waited for me on the other side.

A nature scene with trees and wildlife unfolded before my eyes. I was extremely pleased with the card because the outdoors is close to my heart. I knew there must be another meaning, a symbolic meaning. These meanings were always elusive to me. I struggled to separate the literal sense of meanings from their symbolic counterparts. I felt like I was learning a whole new language that eluded my current level of comprehension, and it frustrated me.

The instructor had been gathering handbooks while we finished with the cards and then provided each of us with a copy. Finally I had a handbook to look at and guide me. In my Native American-style class, there was never a handbook. We went through the material and were reaching the point of applying what we had just learned. I felt the anxiety building in my heart. Was I going to put my hands on someone, or walk out the door? The choice was mine. What should I do?

I dug deep within my soul to find strength. I hopped up on the table and got comfortable. If I could relax enough, I might have a chance to work on another person. My classmate worked on me and I felt extremely relaxed. Now it was my turn to work on her.

I slid off the table and waited for her to climb up and get comfortable. My hands shook and my heart pounded. The anxiety gnawed at my stomach, and I asked the instructor if we should ground ourselves. Grounding always relaxed me, but I had not heard anything in this class about the benefits of grounding. She said we didn't have to ground ourselves, which confused me because we always did in the other class I took.

Listening to my intuition, I grounded myself because that helped me reconnect to the earth's energy. The anxiety in my heart subsided, and my hands began to feel hot—so hot in fact I had to stop and shake them off many times. I asked the instructor many questions as she guided each of the groups through the training.

Working toward my classmate's feet, I felt a huge amount of energy waiting to be released there. We were instructed to stand in front of the feet, which didn't feel comfortable to me because in my other class we were taught to stand to the side of the person's feet. This is important, because once the energy gets released, you don't want that energy getting all over you.

The session went extremely well, and my partner felt relaxed. This was a successful healing day.

In learning two different healing modalities, I observed that the principles were very similar yet applied differently. The energy class from The Center felt focused on an in-depth way of working with energy, and reiki felt more like a conscience flowing of energy to where it needed to go. I feel the unification of holistic healing practices and the vast knowledge that each holds could bring about immense positive working relationships in the healing field.

High Vibrations

Journal Entry 9

*N*ow that I had met with Kate, I was able to continue with class. Once again a vision came. I saw myself and Derrick in class, the seat Chloe always sat in, empty. I knew what was going to happen—Chloe and I would not be together in class anymore—and that made me extremely sad.

The door to the vision I had been given earlier of Chloe moving into my home had also opened, and I had a feeling the mystery of the vision would reveal itself soon.

"Jen, I met this guy Adam at the bookstore." She couldn't contain her excitement on the other end of the phone.

What? I thought.

"I was lead to the spiritual section of the bookstore, and there was a guy standing in the aisle. He removed a book on animal guides and then started talking to me about penguins." Her words spilled through the phone.

"I thought of you, Jen, and I said to him, 'I have a friend who's into animal totems.'" She was excited by the connection.

I had an unsettling feeling deep within my heart about Chloe and Adam's meeting, and I wanted to understand more about my feelings to their connection. I felt compelled to visit Chloe one morning, so I called and made arrangements for a visit.

I arrived midmorning and took a seat on her couch. Chloe began to fill in the details about her meeting with Adam and her phone buzzed. She picked it up.

"He's on his way." She was giddy while wildly texting him back. "He'll be here in five minutes." Her excitement spilled into the room.

I was extremely apprehensive to meet Adam. Where did he come from, and what did he want with her?

Chloe looked out the living room window as my mind wandered. "He's here, Jen!" She was excited.

Adam walked in the front door. Our eyes kept darting back and forth; we could not make or sustain eye contact. We exchanged pleasantries and he sat on the couch between Chloe and me. I was trying to get a read on Adam. He was nervous and a little unsettled about something.

"I have a message for you," he said, looking toward me and then at the floor.

A message from whom and from where? I looked around the room and only saw the three of us. Now he was making me nervous.

"Okay." I was uncertain about what he was talking about.

He slid off the couch and stood in front of me. "Stand up and look into my eyes."

I started to make jokes because I was nervous.

I glanced at Chloe and knew in my heart she would never put me in harm's way. I trusted her.

"It's okay, Jen," she said.

I looked him in the eyes. He clapped his hands in front of me and then jumped on the couch behind me.

I stood quietly on the living room floor. My mind reached as far as it could into its memory banks of experiences. There was no memory file that could be recalled and pulled into an answer for this experience.

Adam lightly tapped me between my shoulder blades and hopped off the couch. "It's all done." He smiled.

The experience was bizarre yet interesting. I asked what he did and he explained that my guides (I wondered what those were) had shown him that I needed a bit of energy work done. Energetically I was having trouble moving forward with many situations in my life. Adam was guided to put my energy back into place, and that's what he did. The idea of energy and guides was a foreign concept to me, and each new puzzle piece confused me more.

The three of us walked into the study area, and Chloe started to pack some of her belongings. Adam had to leave for work and hugged Chloe good-bye. I felt an immense amount of love between them when they hugged; the feeling was incredible. Chloe became quite serious after Adam left, and her seriousness made me anxious.

"Please, Jen," was all she said as her brown eyes locked on mine.

Fear raced through my veins and landed in my heart with the utterance of those two very simple words. I just knew deep within the darkness of my soul that I had to continue forward on a path and along a journey I did not understand or even remember. I wanted desperately to move forward with whatever it was I was forgetting to do, but I didn't know what I was moving toward. I felt like I had lead weights in my feet, afraid to step into an unfamiliar world. I intuitively knew she was saying, "Come on, you can move forward; you can open to a world of possibilities; don't be afraid of the unknown."

I was frightened to take that leap. I had a choice to make, and no one else could make it for me. Could I move forward and push through the fear, or would I crumble and stay lost forever? I wasn't sure.

"Okay." My eyes never left hers. I had just committed myself to move forward with a new path in my life, and I was scared.

It was time for me to head home. I hugged Chloe good-bye and made my way outside. The air was cold, and ice covered the driveway. Thoughts of the day were endlessly replaying in my mind. I couldn't make any sense out of anything. I felt stuck in place but wanted to break free and see what was waiting for me through all the darkness. I had to push through no matter how much struggle it took. Where was I pushing to? I had no clue.

Within a week, my thoughts had quieted down.

"Jen, I need to move in with you." Chloe was ready for a change.

The maternal nature in me took over. "The room is ready anytime you are."

I explained to my family that Chloe was definitely moving in with us so be prepared.

Our first order of business was to go to Chloe's apartment and pick up her belongings. Early one morning, we set out on our moving adventure. Adam was going to meet us at the apartment. When we pulled into her driveway, Adam was already waiting in his car. Chloe went inside the apartment before us, and I chatted with Adam in the driveway. He and I made our way toward the side door.

Upon entering the kitchen, I saw Chloe packing some of her clothes.

"Jen, go clear the kitchen." Chloe handed me a shell, white sage, and matches.

"Okay," I said, wondering how I was going to handle this.

I grabbed the matches, shell, and sage and walked into the kitchen. The air was heavy and thick. I lit the sage, and smoke engulfed the room. I was working with the sage to cleanse the kitchen of negative energy. When I was finished, the room was light and airy, which meant it was now clear and in a better place, one of positive love. I continued through the other sections of the apartment.

"Okay, I'm finished. What's next?" I asked, looking around.

Chloe handed me blue bins and pointed toward the living room. "Start filling these totes."

I filled each tote to the top and packed them into the car. After moving as much as I could, I sat on the couch and watched Chloe and Adam pack. I had never seen anything like it. They were feeling the energy on every piece of clothing, which fascinated me. The pieces that did not feel right were put aside for recycling.

Time flew, and I had to get home and unload the car before the school bus arrived. As I grabbed one more item to stuff into the car, I felt a wave of sadness come over me. My time with Chloe at this apartment was done. This had been our meeting place, the place from which we drove to class together where we laughed, cried, and shared our lives; I thought it was all ending.

As I walked out of the side door to the car, tears streamed down my cheeks.

"What's wrong, Jen?"

I turned around; Adam and Chloe were standing on the back stoop.

"Nothing." I turned away; I didn't want them to see me cry.

They walked toward the back of my car.

"I'm not taking her away from you," Adam said, rubbing the back of my jacket.

"I know." The tears kept flowing.

Chloe and I had a bond. We had experienced so much together, and life was changing yet again. I was struggling to move forward because change was scary as hell. I liked things just the way they were, and to break out of my comfort zone was hard. I hugged them good-bye and headed home.

Adam brought Chloe to my home later that evening, and he decided to hang out with us. I was starting to see a pattern; every major shift in my life involved my husband being called away to work. My husband didn't have the understanding of the changes bombarding my life, so I was being provided time and space for experiencing a higher level of consciousness and learning to deal with my intuitive gifts.

I felt like I was living a double life, one as wife and mother and one a closet intuitive. The vibration in my home was becoming stronger and stronger, and that was because the love that surrounded my family and friends was growing. One evening as I slept, an intense amount of happiness danced in my stomach. I knew it was coming from Chloe in the upstairs bedroom, and I was beginning to notice how another person's emotions could affect me physically.

I reached for my phone on the nightstand. I typed, "I feel your excitement." I could barely see the keyboard from the intensely bright light.

"Oh, geez, I'll ground myself and see if that helps." I felt the giggles in her text.

"Better." I felt calm and fell back to sleep with the phone on my chest.

One afternoon, Chloe and I were sitting in the kitchen. I had asked her to write a book with me and showed her some of my work.

"This isn't right," she said, pushing one of the stories away. "What have you been avoiding?"

I was thinking about all the things I had done in my life, and the one thread that popped into my head was writing.

"Writing?" I questioned.

"You have to write a story about yourself." She was intent on making the point stick.

"But I'm not interesting." I looked at her in disbelief.

"Your story will be inspirational and help others, and then and only then will all the other stories flow, but your window is short." She was receiving the information from her guides, which always startled me. I was learning that guides protect and give guidance when needed to keep us safe and on our paths.

I felt a wave of fear flow through me again. What did I know about writing an inspirational book? I'd read many well-written inspirational books, and I couldn't compete with any of them. What could I say that hadn't been said before? I had started but not finished many stories for teens; an inspirational book was not on my to-do list of books to write.

"You need to start writing, but first you have to work on yourself. Make a list of one hundred questions. By the time you get to eighty-five, the true essence of your questions will start to flow. You will also discover the starting point for the book within those questions."

Great, I had to start writing a book on who knows what to inspire people. I kept telling myself I had nothing to offer. Where would I start? How would I find things to write about? Where would I get an editor, a publisher? I couldn't stand the constant battle in my brain, so I decided to work on the hundred questions right away. I found a binder and filled it with paper. I told my family I needed to be alone to write and please don't disturb me unless there was an emergency. I ran upstairs into the spare bedroom and locked the door. I crawled up on the bed, fluffed the pillows behind my head, and laid there. Now what? I let my mind drift away, and whatever flowed in, I wrote down in the notebook that rested on my chest. For weeks I wrote, and the writing began to release pent-up emotions. I cried for months and then began to analyze the relationships I had over the years and the purposes of each. I saw that each relationship had a lesson to be learned.

For example, my childhood was great, and my parents did a good job raising me. I began to see I absorbed into my own belief system things they feared. This was the key to one of my lessons in this lifetime. The kind of fear I am referring to is the what-if game. I could "what if" myself all day long and worry myself crazy with endless obscure possibilities over worst-case scenarios of things that never happened. Now that I was aware of this strong emotion, how could I work through it?

Life was exciting with Chloe in the house. My intuitive abilities were starting to awaken. My world was expanding, and I was learning how to work on a higher level of consciousness. I was discovering parts of me that I never knew existed. With this expanded awareness came a drive to experience and learn more. My heart bubbled over with gratitude for the guidance and experiences Chloe had shared with me. She was teaching me a lot about how the universe worked, and I was open to learning. Spirit had shown me the vision of Chloe moving in for a reason. It was to prepare me for a change and to get ready. My home became the classroom of a new life.

During this time, my family was noticing significant changes in my demeanor. I was changing the way I thought about the world around me. My beliefs and attitudes were shifting, and that made my family uneasy. My daughter even said she wanted her old mommy back. The tension in our home was rising, and soon Chloe and my work would be coming to an end at my home.

My husband was impatient with the two of us; Chloe and I felt his tension growing. I was aware that I was changing, and my family and friends thought I was having a midlife crisis. I felt pressure from my family to stay the same, but I just couldn't. I knew deep in my heart that there was something more, something else I needed to do in this lifetime, and I couldn't stop until I found the answer. My consciousness had now expanded, and with that, the view of the world I had previously known had shifted. I could no longer walk in the illusionary world I once knew.

The unspoken emotional anxiety between Chloe and my husband was mounting. We both knew it was time for her to move out, and I was sad our time together was almost over. Adam's parents invited Chloe to move into their home, and she took them up on the offer.

Late one evening as I sat on the bed in Chloe's room watching her and Adam pack, I noticed she was highly agitated because she was picking up on my husband's thoughts. I learned at that moment how easy it was for intuitive people to know what others are feeling and thinking about them.

Once the packing was done, we made our way downstairs. It had only been seven days that she was with us, but it seemed much longer than that. Chloe and Adam tiptoed into my daughter's bedroom to say good-bye, then I walked them to the front door.

"What am I feeling when I hug you?" I asked Adam.

"That's love, Jen." He smiled and then walked down the steps.

Mystery of Fire

Journal Entry 10

When visiting family and friends, inferences would sometimes flow through our conversations about particular occupations that related to past lives. However, I never really gave the topic much thought until I started class, and then I began to wonder if the fears I carried could be connected to past-life experiences.

One of my biggest fears was my husband leaving me. Our relationship was comfortable and loving; he never gave me any reason to believe he would ever leave. The fear of my life partner leaving left an undercurrent of emotions I couldn't quite pinpoint. I felt anxious and frustrated that the source of this fear was eluding me. These emotions would sometimes flare as anger. The endless loop of the emotional roller coaster was enough to make me search for answers, and the answer was about to be unlocked.

Once a month, The Center invites the general public in the form of a gathering. One of Kate's very first students, Carol, was hosting a past-life regression class. Space was limited, and I wanted answers that were buried within my heart, so I booked early.

The day of the gathering came, and excitement bubbled through me. Chloe and I had made arrangements to drive together, and her mom, Rebecca, and Adam would be joining us. When we arrived, The Center was bursting with people. We shared great conversations and food, and then everyone took a seat in the gathering room. Chloe sat to the left of me and Rebecca to my right. Chloe was already an instrumental part of my life, and Rebecca would be entering my world six months later as a friend and teacher. We got settled in and waited for instructions.

The anxiety raced through my body as Carol described the hypnosis process and what we might experience. My head was looping with fear, doubt, and wild expectations about how I thought things might be experienced. How was I going to remember what I saw? How did I know this was really what I was experiencing? I couldn't shut my brain off. The anxiety was pulsing through my body, and I was shaking inside.

Carol slowly began to take us through the hypnosis process. I started to relax a little, but not completely. I was determined to figure out how this worked and was keeping one ear open at all times. As Carol led us back in time through this lifetime, visions started to appear as if I was right back in my childhood. I had forgotten about those great times, and it made me feel happy, yet sad those times were gone.

As she led us further back in time, I noticed the landscape starting to change. It was a very hot, dry climate with dirt all around me. Staring at my legs, I saw to my surprise they were the legs of a man. My feet were bare, and I wore a long, tan-colored robe. My head was covered with the same type of material to keep the sun from burning my scalp. I held a long wooden pole with metal on the end, which was used for stonemason work. Not far from where I was working, my camel, my main mode of transportation, waited patiently.

In the distance I saw a fire, and I knew deep within my soul that my wife had been killed. Children ran around all over the desert sand, and tears streamed down my face. Slowly we were brought back through time to the present. As I wiped away the tears, I had the answers to the questions I sought. The fear of my husband leaving me in this life may have been from the death of my wife from a past life.

I pondered the past-life regression for days. Could I have possibly lived before? Why did I live before, and what were these memories that clung to me like heavy, wet clothing? I analyzed every angle I could think of but couldn't fit it into any context of my current life. The struggle to accept the experience frustrated me. Although I had asked for an answer and received one, accepting it was another matter entirely. In order to move forward in my life, I had to release the pain of the energy that remained blocked within my heart. I decided I could no longer carry that pain within me. I acknowledged the sorrow and then, let it go. The emotional weight dropped from my body to the earth. I was no longer captive to that emotional block anymore.

I was liberated from one specific fear that held me within its energetic grasp for so long. Because that one fear was connected to the past, I wondered how many more were locked inside me, driving my emotional state of being. I needed to find the answers that might possibly guide me to an understanding of who I was and why I was living on Earth.

Spirit Boy

Journal Entry 11

Chloe and I were hanging out one evening and decided to pick up her boyfriend, Adam, who worked at a local coffee shop. As we caught up with one another, a young boy of about thirteen appeared on the side of a busy road riding his bike around nine o'clock on a school night. My friend became highly animated, jumping up and down in her seat.

"You saw him, the boy on the bike!" Her face lit up.

"Yeah, I saw him." *What's the big deal?* I thought shrugging.

"He's a ghost, a spirit." Chloe knew what he was because she has the ability to see the differences between the worlds of spirit and human existence.

I saw him as clear as I saw the two of us. I noticed the car behind the boy was so close to hitting his back tire that I swerved in case the boy got hit. The lights of the car did not illuminate the boy in the darkness, and that caught my attention because I thought it odd. The experience reached me on a soul level, and I was not afraid of what I saw or felt. We were both the same, except I had a body and he did not.

We arrived at the coffee shop and gave Adam the details about what we had encountered. He explained that some years ago a young boy had drowned in the river close to where we had seen the spirit boy. The experience motivated me to find the significance of the sighting. What purpose did it serve, and why was it shown to both of us? I constantly thought about the sighting, but experience taught me to just wait and let the scenario play out. Patience was something I needed to learn in dealing with the spirit world.

During this time, my sister and her family were trying unsuccessfully to install a pool. Everything that could possibly go wrong did. I got the feeling the pool shouldn't go up, so I shared this story with Chloe.

"Who can't swim?" she asked me without hesitation.

"My nephew, Patrick, sinks like a brick," I explained.

"The pool shouldn't be installed until he has swimming lessons." Her tone was sincere.

"Okay, I'll let my sister know." I was apprehensive about how to explain the message to my sister, Abbey, without scaring her to death. The next day I gathered enough nerve to pick up the phone and call Abbey.

"I don't want to freak you out, but I've got to tell you something. This isn't from me … but Patrick needs swimming lessons before the pool is installed."

I waited anxiously for a response.

"Okay." I could hear the hesitation in her voice. Almost as if to say, "I understand what you're telling me … but how do you know this?"

This was the first time I had to relay a message from the spirit world to the physical world. The execution on my part was a bumbling mess because I wasn't sure how to convey the message in a tactful way. I was afraid she would think I had totally lost my mind. I knew in my heart that if I didn't speak up, my nephew's safety in the pool could be disastrous, and I wouldn't be able to live with myself if I didn't quickly convey the message.

As I lay in bed one morning thinking about the experience, an "ah-ha" moment seeped into my consciousness. The spirit boy revealed himself because he had drowned in the physical world. The story of his drowning came from Adam to connect the story to the sighting. I had experienced "knowing" the pool should not be installed yet. Then sharing the experience with Chloe who knew swimming lessons were necessary. This was a synchronistic pattern of paying attention to the signs all around us. Because of the assistance of the spiritual and physical worlds working together from a state of love, Patrick was given a gift: life.

Nature Is Healing

Journal Entry 12

*I*t had been about a month since I had successfully completed the reiki course and had a certificate of completion. Reiki was over and Chloe had moved out, which left me in a place of uncertainty. I wasn't sure what to do next or where to go. The door that had been opened for my growth seemed to have shut. I felt empty and alone and was extremely sad she had gone. The only thought that crossed my mind was to walk outside, which I did. Taking a long, slow breath of air and holding it within my lungs, I slowly released the emptiness and sadness from my body and the peacefulness settled in; I wanted to feel like this always. Instinctively, I turned to nature for help.

I sat outside for hours, writing, pouring my heart and soul onto the pages of my journal. Any passing thought that came through my mind became part of the writings. I began to notice a relationship between my thoughts and nature; the two somehow interacted together, and I was noticing. Imagine a thought casually passing through your consciousness and at that exact same moment a hawk, owl, or crow appears in your line of vision. The more I paid attention, the more wild birds and animals appeared. One day I was out shoveling horse manure and heard in my head, "Book Den." I knew this was a local bookstore, so I put the scooper away and climbed into my car.

This is crazy, I thought, fixing my hair in the rear-view mirror.

This was going to be an interesting morning. As I backed out of the driveway, my phone buzzed. It was my husband texting. I put the car in park and waited.

The yellow message bubble beckoned my attention. "What are you up to?"

"I'm headed to a bookstore," I replied, talking into the voice recorder.

The yellow bubble popped back in. "What are you looking for?"

The phone was close to my mouth as I responded. "I'm not sure, but I need to go there."

The other end was quiet. I felt he was trying to make sense of the strange answer I had given him.

"I hope you find what you're looking for," the yellow bubble answered and then was gone.

I arrived before the bookstore opened. *This is crazy,* I thought. *What am I doing here?* I was getting anxious waiting for the store to open. After watching the flag get hung out and a cart of books slowly getting wheeled outside for patrons to purchase, the door opened for business.

I hopped out of the car and wandered inside. It was amazingly large and comfortable. This had now turned from nervous energy into an adventure and I was game. I wandered the isles amazed at the extensive collection of all types of genres spread out before my eyes. I ended up in the Native American section. Adam had told me exactly where this section was located a month or so earlier and I thought that interesting. I perused the shelves.

What am I looking for? I asked in my head.

Bottom shelf. Okay, now my mind was answering me. I must be losing it.

I looked on the bottom shelf and there it was, *The Essential Guide to Native American Healing,* by Kenneth Cohen. I knew this was what I was sent to get. I found another book that looked good to read, so I removed it from the shelf and headed to the register.

I was a little nervous standing at the counter because I had two books that were not your average, everyday, housewife's reading material. The woman at the counter was not very talkative but managed to comment on the material I was purchasing.

"Interesting reading," she remarked.

"Yes it is." I didn't know what else to say.

I gathered up the books and headed out the door. All the way home I wondered what I needed to know. When I arrived home, I headed outside and started reading. Everything I was currently learning in class was being reinforced in the book. There were times I had just read what we would be doing in the next class. I was beginning to see a pattern. How was this possible? My mind was bending again.

One evening while I was writing in the upstairs bedroom, I heard our horse pacing and snorting in the paddock. The chickens decided to get in on the action and started squawking. I tossed my writing materials on the sheets and jumped off the bed. I ran downstairs in my pajamas, passing my sleeping husband sprawled along the couch. My daughter was oblivious in the other room as she watched TV. I hit the latch on the door, stumbled into my muck boots, and ran across the patio to the yard.

"Oh, shit!" I yelled, making a U-turn, heading back to the house.

As I grabbed the handle to the door, I yelled, "Get up! We've got a bear in the chicken coop!" The adrenaline rushed through my body.

My husband flew off the couch and darted out the door.

"Where, where is it?" He looked toward the coop.

I turned around, stepping onto the patio. It had disappeared.

"It was by the side of the fence. It's a black bear!" I wasn't moving any further.

My husband got some metal shovels and smacked them together to make noise, but we couldn't see where the bear had gone. The horse was ready to charge the fence, so we knew it was close. I carefully walked to the horse and donkey, watching their body language for any signs of shift in their attitudes, and then climbed the fence. I approached the donkey, who was as close to the fence rail as she could get. The horse wouldn't budge from her spot, looking straight at the coop. I was trying to follow her line of vision but still couldn't see anything. Moments later the horse began to circle me and the donkey; she was protecting her herd, which included me.

I watched as my husband slowly walked through the yard toward the coop. My heart was pounding, my nerves jumping.

"Get your ass back to the house!" he yelled as he ran through the yard.

My body jolted forward. Before realizing it, I was flying through the air, my feet landing on the ground. My arms and legs were moving rapidly as I turned to look over my right shoulder. Could I outrun a black bear?

We both made it safely to the back porch.

"Where is it?" I gasped for air.

"It's behind the coop." He reached for the door handle.

Seconds later he came back with his bow and arrow.

"You can't shoot it!" I shrieked, worried about the bear's safety.

"I'm not going to shoot it, just scare it way!" he bellowed, rapidly heading for the back lawn.

The daylight was fading fast. The first arrow took off whizzing through the air. We heard it land someplace deep in the dense forest. The second arrow spun off. Bam, it hit the wood on the coop, and I heard it ricochet into the darkening forest. There was only silence now, but the horse and donkey were still alert and unmoving. The bear was still there. We lit the tiki torches and turned on the spotlight, which illuminated the backyard. We anxiously watched over the livestock for two more hours. A friend of ours had shown up to help out with our furry guest and we all kept our distance; no one wanted an altercation. Finally we heard the branches and twigs being crushed underneath the weight of the bear's feet as it walked off our land and deeper into the dark forest. The horse and donkey were no longer on high alert as they followed the sound of the bear leaving into the night. We kept the spotlight on all evening, and thankfully the night remained quiet. I was amazed that every person we shared our story with said the bear would be back. I intuitively felt in my heart that this encounter was meant for me and the bear was not coming back anytime soon. I wasn't sure of the true essence the bear encounter would reveal.

All through the seasons an abundance of animal visitors crossed my path, and I was paying attention to their presence. An opossum had been locked in the chicken coop by my daughter one night. When I opened the door in the morning, two little black eyes looked at me from behind the feed can. I wondered how I could remove the opossum without either one of us getting hurt when a quick flash of our cat carrier popped into my mind. "That's a clever idea," I said out loud and ran inside to fetch it. Upon returning to the coop, I moved the feed can and placed the cat carrier in front of the opossum. Gently tapping the opossum on its backside with a stick, it went inside the carrier. I tromped through the deep snow, wondering where and how to remove it from the carrier. I found a fallen tree and thought it would make a great hiding place for the critter. Carefully unlatching the door, I tipped the carrier over and lightly tapped the back end. The opossum slid out onto the tree, scurrying underneath it.

One night as I was lounging, I heard little tiny steps on the back porch. I knew the cat was out, so I opened the door. I kept calling for him but he wasn't responding, so I shut the door and went to flip on the porch lights. Jake the cat had suddenly turned into a white skunk with a black strip down his backside. I slowly backed away, talking softly to the skunk, and shut the door. I respectfully watched the skunk leave the porch into the darkness, and then Jake appeared from the darkness in the other direction. Luckily he missed this encounter as he had been sprayed a few years earlier.

I drove home one night to find a peacock standing in the middle of the road. Once I stopped, it looked at me and then proceeded on its way. A few months later the same bird flew across my path on the same road in the same spot. I slammed on the brakes, and the passengers went flying forward. We almost had bird for dinner that night.

One of the most amazing encounters occurred while I was driving in a nearby town. My attention was pulled to the driver's-side window. I saw something large heading straight for my windshield and I flinched. A large, red-tailed hawk soared out of the tree line, its right side gliding straight for the front windshield. I looked into its big dark eye in awe, which was a beautiful moment, a precious gift.

Early one morning I was sitting in the woods deep in thought. My two cats were rubbing all over me and suddenly stopped. I watched their eyes and followed their gaze into the woods. I heard a loud snap and we all froze. Appearing before our eyes was a beautiful black bear. I sat in awe watching this big powerful animal stroll through the forest. It was maybe fifty feet from me and didn't seem to notice my existence. After I realized this was not television, I slowly got up and backed away. The cats had hightailed it out of the area long before I did.

My husband remarked on what he had been observing to some friends of ours one evening. He commented about the unusual amount of animal visitors we were receiving. I chuckled because I was beginning to see and understand the connections myself. The animals and birds that were out of their usual day-to-day activities were making their presence known in a big way, and I was listening. They were sending me messages. Now I had to learn how to understand and apply the messages to my life.

I began to remember how much I had loved to be in the woods as a kid. I was always climbing trees, throwing crabapples, picking pears, making magic potions with poisonous plants, and making mud pies. I see now why I love to be in the garden. Plant a seed, water, and care for it. Watch it grow like my own child. Then it blooms into a beautiful harvest. Our lives are very much connected to nature, yet at some point I seemed to dismiss it as separate from myself.

As I began to reconnect with nature, I made a conscious decision to go hiking as much as possible during the year. Luckily, my sister, Abbey, and her family love the forest as much as I do, and we set out on many adventures. One morning we set out for the old town of Dana. This was a town that was moved to put in the Quabbin Reservoir. The day was warm and the sky clear. We loaded my nephews' backpacks with lunches and waters and hiked the two-and-a-half miles into the old town. The scenery was beautiful. We chatted and laughed all the way to what was once the center of town. The buildings and homes had all been torn down. The only signs of the town's existence were dirt roads, stone foundations, and plaques that told a brief story of what once stood before us. We found a spot where the old school once held the hopes and dreams of the town's children. It was a peaceful spot to rest and eat our lunch. I knelt with one knee in the grass and faced the breeze so my hair would not get eaten with my sandwich. My nephew, Patrick, was staring at me.

"Auntie, you look kind of pretty, like in a movie with the wind in your hair." The honesty flowed from his heart.

"Thanks, buddy," I said with love in my heart. He had touched a cord deep within my soul and it moved me. He saw the beauty that resided within me.

We finished our lunch and packed up our trash. While walking toward the giant stacked-stone foundation that once held a hotel in place, I noticed the plaque and the stunning picture of the old structure. My sister joined me, and we discussed various aspects of the landscape.

Then an idea crossed her mind. "I wonder where the water is from here." She was curious to find a direction for us to hike.

The words had just left her mouth when I noticed a teenage boy with a fishing pole and full fishing gear walking on the dirt road about thirty feet to our left.

"I guess we will follow that kid with the fishing pole." I pointed at the boy walking by.

We gathered ourselves and the backpacks, making our way to the dirt road to follow the boy with the fishing gear.

"Auntie, will you come get my stick with me? I left it over there." Patrick pointed to the spot we just ate our lunch.

"Okay, but let's be fast." I scanned the area to see where the boy had gone.

Patrick picked up his stick, and then I sent him to the family while I headed to the Porta-Potty. I hurried so we could catch up with the boy. We walked at a brisk pace, but we could not find where the boy went. The road was dirt, and I was looking for footprints or dust trails, anything to give us an indication as to what path he might have taken to get to the water. The kids were beginning to get tired of walking and the whining began. Suddenly we heard a giant snap in the woods. We all stopped and looked at each other and then looked into the forest behind us.

"What was that?" my brother-in-law, Mike, asked.

I could see no movement in the forest. We said nothing to each other, but our feet all picked up the pace as we quickly walked away from the area. Within ten minutes the kids were done, physically tired and mentally drained. We turned around and headed back toward the town and the car. It felt like someone was walking behind us, and I kept glancing behind me, but no one was there. I noticed Mike doing the same thing. We stopped and rested for a while as everyone was fatigued. The road behind and the road ahead were peacefully quiet. There was not a soul around except for the six of us. We made our way back to the parking area, which was about a six-mile roundtrip hike by foot that day; we were all exhausted.

"I have to use the bathroom; I'll be right there." Abbey stopped at the Porta-Potty and the rest of us continued on toward the car.

She met up with us a short time later.

"Did you see the kid with the fishing pole? He walked passed me by the bathroom headed toward the car." She looked a bit confused.

I connected the pieces of the story together to form my conclusion. The boy appeared in our line of vision when my sister asked where the water was. Then as we went to follow him, his trail disappeared. The road we walked on stretched unobstructed in both directions for a very long distance. We could clearly see that no one was in front of or behind us during our entire hike. On the trip back to the car, I kept hearing footsteps behind me, yet no one was physically there. Abbey stopped at the bathroom. When she was finished and left the bathroom, the boy with the fishing gear walked by her headed in the direction of where the car was parked. None of us saw him walk by as we waited for her. I didn't say anything in front of the kids because they got spooked really easily. We piled into the car and headed for home.

When we arrived at my house, I asked Abbey if she would be okay in knowing who the fishing boy was.

"Okay," she said hesitantly.

"He was a spirit, leading us to the water," I calmly stated.

"Oh," she said.

That was the end of the conversation. That was two messages I had relayed to my sister from the spirit world in a very short amount of time. I was so preoccupied with conveying the messages to her that I hadn't noticed she too could see spirit people. She just wasn't aware of it yet. I was beginning to understand that spirit people revealed themselves when necessary to guide and support us, and I was interacting on this level more often than I was aware of.

As I began to work with nature and build a relationship with Earth, I was seeing I was connected in a web vaguely visible before. I had felt a void in my life and struggled to find what that void was. It was nature and my interconnectedness to the very world I deeply appreciated.

I love to garden and know soil is alive and rich with tangible creatures that I can physically see, such as worms and beneficial insects. I also know compost creates a soil that is rich in organic material that boosts the growing potential of the plants. I can't see the chemical compounds contained in the soil or the microbes that live there, but science has made an awareness of these living organisms. I have learned by observing nature and being taught by my mother and friends that as the earth seasons and cycles, so do we. For example, the leaves that fall from the trees provide protection and cover for the life that remains on the floor of the earth. As the leaves break down, the soil gets fed all on its own without our help to regenerate itself.

That being the case, I began to wonder why humans feel the need to control and guide nature. The natural world has been cycling for millions of years without human interference. As the forests are removed from that natural cycle, I can't but help think we will become extinct, just as many animals have become, if we don't wake up and become aware of our actions and their effect on the natural world, it seems to be that simple. You and I as the collective whole of society need to pay attention to our actions in regard to how we work with the land and all that share the space together. We are all responsible for our part in living *with* the earth, not *on* the earth.

I now understand the animals were trying to get my attention so I would notice the world around me. My guides worked through nature, especially animals, because that's what I was most comfortable accepting as guidance. I connected well to nature and the energy of the animals that presented themselves to me.

I find nature not only healing but vital for our survival on many levels. Once I began to reconnect with the natural world and experience the beauty that lay within that world, I began to see the link that nature provided to me and all of us. In order to sustain ourselves, we need to sustain her. Nature has proven herself to regenerate from destruction after destruction; she does not thrive with us upon her, but we must have her to thrive and survive. I was beginning to see how small humans were in the web of life.

Spirit of the Orchard

Journal Entry 13

Autumn is my favorite season. The vivid colors of leaves beckon attention by dancing gently upon the breeze, waiting to be seen as the beautiful spirits they are. This is especially true of apple-picking season. I love to walk through the rows of trees and tall grass while admiring the clouds as they float above me, like giant pillows waiting to be jumped on and ridden across the sky.

One day as I was out with Chloe. We were driving deep into the woods, winding our way through the back roads of a small town near her home. We came upon a very old apple orchard and barn.

"I've got to go there one day." I was so impressed with the size and cleanliness of the building.

"They make really great pies here," she happily explained.

My wish to visit the orchard was to be granted a few months later. I had recently made friends with Rebecca and her daughter, Kaia. Our girls were the same age, and we had a lot of fun together. We made plans to go apple picking, and I was extremely excited to show her this new place.

I was learning that adventures with Rebecca were just as interesting as adventures with Chloe. We set out early one September morning for our apple-picking adventure. We never knew what to expect, and that was always intriguing.

"This is going to be a spirit-filled day," Rebecca commented.

I wonder what that means. I glanced over and smiled at her.

The few trips we had been on together seemed to be energetically guided, which always led us on a different path than we had intended. I was learning that when we listened to our intuition to guide us, the beauty that lies just beyond our current awareness would reveal itself. This trip would push me to a new level of that awareness.

We arrived at the orchard to a parking lot filled with happy children and frazzled parents. We began our search for the apple bag pickup booth by following the crowds. Once we paid for the bags, we made our way through the orchard. The kids went one way and we went another. The sky was a vivid blue, with the clouds hanging in the air like fluffy white cotton balls. The light breeze blew through the leaves on the apple trees, enhancing the smell of autumn, which danced into my lungs with each breath. Nature had provided us with a spectacular day, and we were happy to be part of it.

As we walked farther into the orchard, Rebecca and I tried to remember the order of the apple tree varieties and which we would prefer to pick. I was using my intuition to feel my way around the orchard. Rebecca reminded me to ask the tree permission to pick an apple from its branch and then give the tree gratitude for its gift. I had never been apple picking this way before, and I found it to be a respectful and fun learning experience. My awareness became elevated to the connectedness of myself to the trees. Again, nature was teaching me to work with it. We filled our bags as high and wide as the material would stretch, until we ran out of room for more.

"We need to find the girls and bring these to the car," Rebecca said, fumbling with her bag of apples.

"Let's bring ours to the car now and find the girls when we're done," I replied, stuffing my bag of apples into the crook of my left arm.

We meandered our way out of the orchard to the car. After placing the apples in the backseat, we headed back to the orchard.

"How are we going to find the girls in this vast amount of trees?" I asked, scanning the rows and rows of beautiful trees.

"We feel for them using our senses." Rebecca beamed as a smile swept across her face.

"I can do that." I was ready to begin the fun.

We immediately sensed the girls and headed in that direction. Within a few minutes we saw them, and they did what any normal teenage girls would do—ran away from us. We laughed because we could track them with our senses wherever they went, and we had fun finding them in the vast rows of apple trees. After twenty minutes of playing, we proceeded to the barn to get yummy treats. I was about to get a treat I didn't expect.

The barn was swarming with people who made it difficult to maneuver toward the smell of fresh cider doughnuts wafting through the air. We wandered in and out of the nooks and crannies of the barn, stopping to look at handmade crafts, books, and jams, and then my eyes lit up as I saw the most beautiful site: the homemade fudge counter! I was deeply engulfed in the varieties of fudge when Rebecca tapped me on the shoulder, pulling me away.

"Come over here." She was headed to an antique section in the back of the store.

I followed her, leaving the fudge behind, and wham! A rush of energy engulfed my being.

"What is that?" I asked, wiping away and pushing the heavy feeling off my chest. The feeling was intensely uncomfortable, and I felt unsure of how to handle this new sensation.

"That's spirit energy!" Rebecca smiled as she walked away, leaving me alone with the spirit.

No two people feel spirit energy the same way. I usually feel an intense pressure in my heart chakra or energy field, and the feeling is not comfortable. Rebecca feels strong tingles throughout her body and loves the feeling.

As I walked down the narrow isle, the spirit came with me. I looked around the room to see where I could be alone and figure out what to do in this situation. A thought popped in. I spoke to the spirit with my thoughts. *You need to back off me; you're too intense.*

The energy immediately lowered in intensity.

At that moment the girls walked in on me standing alone in the isle.

"You need to go," I said seriously.

"We need the car keys," Kaia said. She was no stranger to spirit energy and wasn't bothered by it.

My daughter, on the other hand, concerned me. I gave them the keys from my coat pocket and got back to communicating with the spirit.

What are you trying to show me? I asked through my mind as to not alert the shoppers in the other isles. They might have wondered why I was talking to the air. I wandered the isles looking for any clue the spirit was trying to lead me to, but what? I rounded the corner and met up with Rebecca.

"There's a message here, but I'm not sure where," I said to her as I looked around the antique-filled tables at the far end of the room.

"It's getting really cold in this spot. That's the spirit's energy," she said, feeling the air with her hands and loving every second of it.

I was beginning to get chilly, which reminded me of the experience with Derrick and Chloe. I glanced up and over to my left. I noticed an enormous antique wall map, which was aged and very brown. This was a map of my town and other surrounding towns. My eyes darted from town to town looking feverishly for a clue. My eyes landed on a town and fixated there.

"Rebecca, that's the town—that's where we need to go." I pointed to a spot on the map.

My mind spun in circles. Where were we supposed to go in that town, and what were we supposed to see? I was always a bit impatient wanting to know what the messages meant. I guessed I would have to wait some more.

Rebecca turned to leave and I followed her out, but the spirit wouldn't leave me alone and followed me down the aisle. I didn't understand what else needed to be seen. I was learning how to deal with spirit energy that I could feel but not see.

I don't know what else you need to show me, I thought, scanning the room looking for a clue, but I was indeed clueless.

I met up with Rebecca and the kids and we exited the back room.

"That was intense." I shook my body like a dog, trying to remove the spirit energy from my being.

"I love that feeling." Rebecca beamed.

The spirit stayed behind when we left. The aromatic smell of cider and doughnuts called to us as we made our way toward the sweet treats. We grabbed a few bags of doughnuts and fudge and then stood in line waiting to pay.

Rebecca noticed a book rack to the right of the register and pointed it out to me. I walked over to read the cover of the first book I saw. It was of the same town the spirit had guided us to. That was two connections of the same town in a span of ten minutes. I knew coincidences were really synchronicities, and we needed to pay particular attention to this town.

After purchasing our cider and doughnuts, we headed back to the car and had a quick tailgate lunch. When we finished, I took Rebecca and Kaia to my house for the afternoon. I loved being with a friend who could discuss great philosophical ideas and to have adventures with. I was beginning to live life with new eyes, and life became amazing. Our adventurous day together was almost over, as it was getting late into the evening and I still had to drive Rebecca and Kaia home to the city.

The day had turned into a clear night. The stars intensely beamed down on us as we drove a long stretch of road toward the city. I decided to open the sun roof and let the night air flow through the car. Rebecca and I were having fun bantering with the girls when a gust of wind that smelled like sage blew in through the sunroof.

"Oh my God, I know what that is," Rebecca said dramatically, looking at the girls in the back of the car. "That's sage," she added, looking through the sunroof.

We sniffed the air, the scent extremely strong. I wondered what the message was, because there must be a message from the world of Spirit.

As we drove closer to the city, we felt a shift in the energy, and it felt heavy and uncomfortable. Arriving at a stoplight, my thoughts drifted off as I starred at the red light. I glanced over to Rebecca, and she wore an odd expression on her face. She turned toward the inside of the car where the girls were sitting, and I began to feel anxious and a bit scared because of her expression. She whispered to me that she would tell me later. I wanted to know what she was talking about, so I hurried to her home as quickly as I could.

We arrived safely, and once the girls were out of hearing range I asked, "What was going on?" I was a bit nervous to hear the answer.

"I turned to look at the girls and saw a giant mass of black energy headed toward the car. I said, 'Oh no you don't.'" Her eyes got larger than usual. Now we understood what the sage was for earlier in the ride.

I felt very uneasy because I now knew dark energy existed in the world and the sage was spiritually gifted to us as protection. On the way home, I was on the lookout for anything unusual. We made it home without any trouble. I was energetically exhausted from the day and needed to crawl into the comfort of my bed. Spirit was providing me with the people, experiences, and knowledge to learn new skills. One long day of adventures took me two weeks to recover energetically.

What Turned upside down for Me

Journal Entry 14

One night in class we were discussing why people don't want to see or acknowledge how the world really operates. I was raised with some beliefs that never sat well with me. I asked many questions about those beliefs, but the answers never made any sense. Why was I following these types of beliefs when my heart wasn't in it? Was it just because my family had for generations? I desperately wanted the truth but did not know where to turn when I was younger.

The tornado had been the wakeup call for the truth I sought. The beliefs I had been taught all those years ago were based on fear and sin. As my journey started to unfold, the beliefs I knew were as far away from the truth as the North Pole is to the South Pole. I had tremendous trouble accepting the truth as it really was. Every single day my mind twisted and thoughts looped endlessly. There were so many thoughts; I had no more room to think. I would shut everything off completely. My heart was bogged down with fear and doubt for leaving the old truths behind. I was walking in a world that couldn't possibly exist. I was now stuck between what I perceived to be real and what I perceived might have existed before. The more I fought the truth, the more emotional strain my mind and body felt. I would have emotionally good and bad days. I felt like I was living on a slingshot that would not stop swinging. All I could feel, taste, smell, and touch was real, but how could I be experiencing all the other senses of an invisible world?

Living with a foot in both worlds—one foot in the physical and one in the spiritual—was a struggle. Being aware of deeper workings within the universe was at the same time fascinating and frightening. I had to be careful with the discussions I had with family and friends. I didn't want to scare them away. Over time, interesting connections started to happen. Some of the stories in this book I began to share with my friends. They understood what I was saying because it was coming from my heart. That's when I realized when the truth is spoken, it is felt on a deeply unconscious level and is accepted. When even the littlest of white lies flows out of our mouths, the heart automatically knows it is not a truth and rejects it.

I also began to see that people who are more sensitive than others can pick up on thoughts, emotions, vibrations in words, and energy fields and just know what others are all about. This felt a little uncomfortable because some people would get to know me on a deeper level than I knew myself. I couldn't lie to myself any more, for that was seen immediately.

So what happened? I had the free will to either move forward on my journey or not. I could freak out over every situation that arose, or I could learn to handle situations in a different way. I began to see how the larger picture of synchronicities worked, and that helped me to remove a lot of the baggage of fear and worry I carried around my neck like a weight. This is the best way I know how to explain the journey I went through for almost two years.

I felt as though I had an energetic tether on my heart, and that tether would get pulled on and fling me like a rubber band by an unseen force. The more I resisted change and acceptance, the more the tether was yanked, and all I could do was run and try to catch up. Of course it wore me down. I would mentally be slammed into trees; the tether would loosen so I could collect myself and wipe the tears from my eyes from the pain. Then, just as everything was quiet, the tether shot me forward again. Only this time, I would fall into a giant dark hole and dangle there waiting for help. Only after I squirmed and flailed for an eternity would the tether loosen as an invisible force pulled me to the surface. For the moment I would catch my breath, and then off we went again until I could take no more. It was run and rest, and I was getting tired. Finally, I began to ask for help and sought inner guidance. And you know what? The tether released from my chest. I became a more experienced version of myself again. That's how my transformation felt to me.

Every now and again, I slip back into old patterns and have to make a conscious effort to be aware of my thoughts. I feel that soon enough these patterns will be completely broken. I trust that I can expand my consciousness to a level where life will just flow peacefully.

As I was lying in bed one morning reflecting on all that I had been through, the next journal entry popped into my head. I knew I had to write it down and share it. This is how I felt during my awakening or remembering of who I was.

Space The Awakening

*F*loating alone through the vast universe, you spot a suit, so you jump into it. It feels awkward and uncomfortable. You look at your hands and feet trying to figure out why you look the way you do.

From the suit you notice a tether, a lifeline connected to an odd gigantic floating piece of metal in space. Without the tether, you would freely float away, aimlessly wandering through the dark void of nothingness with no destination, no plan.

You look off in the distance and see a big blue ball spinning and can't figure out what it is. You are curious to get a closer look but are tethered to this floating apparatus. Confusion sets in on how to unhook yourself and not float away from the "mother ship." You take a chance, your eyes on the big blue ball, and pull the cord loose. You start to drift in the black void, praying you hit your destination. The only way to find out was to let go. The freedom feels uneasy, foreign, as you plummet closer to the big blue ball.

To your surprise you land gently on the surface. You survey your surroundings, never leaving the confines of your suit. As you move, you realize your vision is a bit blurred and the suit starts to become heavier and heavier, almost to the point of being stuck in one place.

You now have to make a choice: start removing the suit, or be stuck in one place forever. The fear and doubt of the unknown world you can't see frightens you. You have drifted alone for so long in the dark abyss. Do you have the faith and trust to move forward? To give up the suit gives up the control, but control of what? Staying lost forever in the darkness?

You made the choice to cut the line and come here, and now you have to make the choice to remove the suit that masks your vision, the only existence you had known for so long.

The choice is instantly made. You rip the arms off the suit, tearing and pulling at them. You begin to regain some movement. *Ah, that feels better.* You move a little further, and your legs feel heavy. If your arms are lighter, what about your legs? You rip the legs from your suit. You feel even lighter. You move forward, but your chest is heavy, full of fear and doubt. If this lightness works for your arms and legs, why would it not work for your chest?

You take a deep breath in the safety of your helmet and pull the chest protection off. It drops to the ground beneath you. The feeling is strange yet pleasant. You're free from the weight. You run, jump, feel, and experience a whole new way. You feel sensations that were locked away for so long, and it feels amazing.

You reach for your face; the helmet is firmly affixed to your head. You want to look and see through the darkened face-shield, but you are afraid. What is out there? The rest of you is free; your head is still a prisoner of the darkness filled with dark thoughts of fear, doubt, and uncertainty. These thoughts keep looping through your head. Why won't they stop torturing you? You know it has to come off. It needs to. You're afraid, so afraid. Will you be able to handle what you see? How will you deal with what you see? The endless loop goes on and on! You slam your fist against the side of the helmet. Stop, stop, stop!

The helmet cracks. A sliver of light breaks through the darkness. It blinds you, making you squint. You try to see. Where does this light come from, and why couldn't you see it before? You hit the helmet a bit gentler, and it cracks some more. More light comes streaming in. You adjust your eyes a bit more. You repeat this pattern over and over until it begins to feel comfortable. You see colors and shades. You smell new aromas, and you become intrigued at what lies beyond the confines of the helmet. You can feel a strange sensation welling up in your chest. It feels exciting. What's holding you back, a prisoner to the new?

You raise both arms, one on each side of your helmet. You gently touch the helmet where your ears are. Slowly you slide your thumbs underneath the openings in the bottom of the helmet. This is it. You take a deep breath, exhaling slowly.

Lifting the helmet with your hands, your arms rise, guiding the process of removing the weight that has held you in the dark for so long. The helmet slides over your ears, rising above the crown of your head. Your eyes are closed. You cradle the helmet in your arms, tucking it into the nook of your elbow like a newborn. Your eyes are tightly shut. You hold on tight to the last bit of the old. You gently kneel, placing your helmet at your feet. You rise, take a deep breath, and open your eyes.

You glance at your surroundings, your head lighter, and your body free. You see a new world free from fear and doubt. You see a world of love and trust. You feel a bit unsteady with your new vision and body. A newness to get use to, free from limited views, free from floating aimlessly, free from the confines of the walls in your mind.

You worked, struggled, crawled, stumbled, and made many mistakes. Now you see the clarity in all that had been masked. You see the truth, the guidance, the world for what it truly is, and you will only move forward, never looking back, because the past is done, never to hold you in its memory again.

You are now truly free to live the way you came here to be.

Who I Am

Journal Entry 16

I often wondered about the universe and my being alone in a vast system of galaxies and universes. How could it be we were the only ones here? This thought had never sat well in my heart. I struggled to learn who I was and what I was doing on Earth. Being guided to The Center was the first step in the process. I was taught a Native American style of life. For me, it is a life that walks with Spirit and nature. Learning this way showed me another way to be. It is a life of peace that is rich in beautiful moments. A life that is unique and equal to all other life forms.

In the past, I held onto material possessions as a way to fill the void I felt inside. The more things I acquired, the emptier I felt. The true beauty was letting things go and replacing those things with truth. My truth is unique and different to me, yet equal and just as beautiful as yours. Because I sought out the answers to my truth, material things are not so valuable to me anymore. A shift occurred in my unconscious awareness, and a broader vision of myself connected me to a greater understanding of who I am.

So, who am I? I am one who is connected to each of you, to the trees, the animals, the stars, and the moon. The earth and all who dwell upon her visible and invisible. I am connected to a vast unseen source known by many names and many cultures. I am a spiritual being living in the physical plain of existence.

I am light, I am dark

I am a breeze on the ocean waves

I am a hawk soaring high
I am laughter that dwells in your soul
I am pain of years untold
I am a whisper that blows by your ear
I am the sunrise
I am the stars
I am peace
I am fear
I am doubt
But most of all, I am truth if you seek me out
Will I follow or be left on my own?
I move forward to figure me out
Know that I love you for all that you are
You are perfect in spite of your scars
I am lifetimes of hurt, sorrow, and pain
I am lifetimes of kindness and soulful gain
I am happy, humble, and grateful for life
I love deeply for all that I am
Who I Am?
I am awake
I am inspiration
I am laughter and joy
I am friendship and fun
I am a lover and mother to one
I am a sister, a daughter, an aunt, and a friend
I am kindness and strength
I am courage and hope
I am the light connected to all
I am equal
I am you and you are me
We are together as one if we choose to be
I am soul who's purple and fluffy
I have come to learn and grow
To share knowledge then go
Go to the light
That's Who I Am

The Winds of Change Spiral Back

The winds of change came back to the beginning of the circle. It had been almost two years of self-analysis, agonizing soul searching, and excruciating reflection on the person I once was to the transformed person who stood before me in the mirror.

I headed to my daughter's high school for parent-teacher conferences at her insistence. I knew this would be the time I would see Amber (the friend I had parted ways with) and would have to make a decision to either talk with or ignore her. After all I had learned, I knew in my heart that I needed to talk with her.

On my way out of the building, I spotted Amber talking with our mutual friend, Violet. I knew what I needed to do.

She was a bit startled to see me walking toward her.

"Hi, how's it going?" I asked with a smile.

"Fine; how are you?" she replied with a puzzled look on her face.

The conversation was a bit awkward but then it started to flow. The feeling of an old comfortable friendship wandered back.

"When can I come see the house?" I happily asked.

"Text me, and we will set a day," she replied with a smile.

I kept my word and texted her a few days later. We set a date, and I arrived on time for our first visit in two years. We had a deep conversation of our separate journeys. We were led down two very different paths that spiraled back around and led us to similar fabrics of truth. We each decided that the drama was over and a peaceful, more relaxed life was unfolding. We had been pulled from the drama of the world into a world of self–reflection, a world where our individual truths had to be dug out of our souls and worked on individually.

I learned I had a tremendous amount of walls that were seen by others, yet I was so unaware of these walls myself. Humor covered my true inner self, the self not wanting to deal with years and numerous lives of hurt and pain. Amber saw these small cracks at times, and I would let her in to see my true being. She saw a depth of thought, compassion, and love where I had seen none. The walls of hurt kept others from getting inside.

For four and a half hours we talked about the paths we were led on, which took us right back to each other. This time we were both aware of our old thoughts and emotions and our reactions to the same. She asked why I had left, and the truth was I couldn't deal with the tragedy and loss from the tornado. She leaned heavily on me and I crumbled. The overload was suffocating as I absorbed every bit of her emotions.

The meeting was healing for both of us. She wanted an understanding of what had happened to our friendship, and I knew I owed her an answer. We learned what was important to one another, without the constraints of expectations placed on us by one another. We had moved past the drama of situations, seeking happiness and a peacefulness that was now within our very core. We wanted to just be who we were and share that with one another. We wanted to have deep and meaningful conversations with substance and compassion while truly listening to the other person's point of view. We let our hearts do the talking, and I learned when the heart speaks, the truth is heard and understood on a very deep level. A reconnection to another person is priceless and worth the struggle and tears.

The tornado was devastating and ripped the very core of our spirits apart, yet it brought us back together in a very peaceful state of existence. It's interesting to look back and see what was missed or misinterpreted. When in so much destruction, the logical brain goes out the window and emotions pulse through the body. Just trying to survive day by day, it feels like a train sitting on your chest with thoughts endlessly looping in despair.

Our growth as people had to undergo this traumatic ordeal in order to transcend walls, blocks, and deep pain. Only then could we see the beauty that is in all things and move forward by living our lives in truth, peace, and harmony. We are once again friends with a new respect for one another. From the destruction and dark came new growth and love.

Conclusions

Journal Entry 18

The last two years of my life have been an adventure that fiction novels are made of. All I wanted was answers, information, and an ending to the many stories I had started writing years ago. The joke was on me when Chloe informed me I had to write about myself. On this quest for knowledge and understanding, I found something more. I found myself wrapped in layers of energetic lifetimes. Grateful for so many mistakes made during this journey, for those very mistakes have taught me valuable lessons that I will share with you. I have reflected often upon my journey, knowing fully well I have a great deal more to learn. If I dare be bold and say I have nothing more to learn, then my growth will falter and I will never truly know the potential that lies within my heart.

My journey was excruciating at times and thrilling at others. My life was so off-balance that I had trouble accepting what I was experiencing. I struggled with a mind that was so confused with new concepts it hurt to think anymore. I felt so alone and wanted desperately to share these experiences with my family, but they were not in the same place of awareness I was. Thankfully I had people to lean on and cry with as we experienced similar journeys.

During this time of awakening, my life seemed to be unraveling in every direction. The company my husband worked for was on the brink of going out of business. Money that once poured into our household slowed to a crawl. A babysitting job came my way, which paid for the classes I was taking at The Center. My family thought I was in the midst of a midlife crisis, although that may have been a lot easier than what I was experiencing. I prayed every day for answers and sometimes fell on my butt in the dirt of the paddock sobbing because the world as I knew it was shifting into a new awareness, and I did not understand what was happening to me.

So what can I share with you about the value of my lessons? Life as I thought I knew it dramatically changed. I learned that the world is evolving faster in the awakening process, and those who are called to read *A Foot in Both Worlds* are awakening as well. My transformation of purpose, or shift in perspective from old beliefs, patterns, and perceptions was swept into a new purpose. A path of conscious awareness was experienced in a more dynamic, respectful way.

I came to an understanding that all life is alive on many levels and it truly never dies; energy is infinite and expands forever. Life is energy, an intelligent consciousness that demands love and respect to be able to work within the scope of this remarkable life force. I also learned that we are all equally held into life by universal or spiritual guidelines. One we hear of often is karma, and it will repeat itself until we learn our lessons from it. We must come to an understanding that our thoughts, actions, and emotions are energy. Everything we say and do has a vibration (a cause and effect). That's why it is so important to keep a positive attitude, even when life beats us down.

I learned my intuition is the guiding force in my life, for it and it alone knows how and where to guide me. My intuition is connected to all things, be it in the physical world or the world of spirit, for it is one and the same energy. I had a tremendously difficult time in accepting and understanding energy. I finally realized I'd had natural abilities my entire life and used them on an unconscious level with positive outcomes. When I began to consciously work with my abilities, that's when I over thought the process and made mistakes. I had no prior frame of reference to connect the why and how of these abilities—why I had them, what the purpose of them was, and how to work with them. I often wondered why not everyone had the experiences I was having. Then I began to see that some of my family and friends did, but they just weren't aware of it on the same level yet.

My journey has made me ponder philosophical questions—not to debate or argue over but to find richer, more fulfilling answers. I wondered what I was trying to attain in life and who set these beliefs in motion in my mind. Were these really my beliefs to begin with or part of a bigger picture? I knew in my heart there was more to myself and the world around me, and material things weren't filling the void when I attained them. There had to be another way, a missing piece to my existence. I kept hearing the term oneness and that which is in all things. Was this what I was searching? The answer is yes. I was looking for the reconnection to my inner spirit and the natural world. I had found the answer to my questions without even realizing it.

You and I truly are the same in our hearts; our minds just haven't caught up with ourselves. We all have innate gifts and intuitive abilities. Some are just more developed than others. It's not something to be in awe of, scared of, or even jealous of; abilities are part of who we inherently are, deep within ourselves. The next time you're sitting around a fire gazing endlessly in wonder and amazement at the stars blazing brightly above in the night sky, quietly ask yourself, *What is my purpose here?* You may be surprised by what you hear.

You and I are all on the journey of life together. We have the choice to struggle through our individual lessons or meet those lessons head on with courage and grace. Sometime I buried my head under my blankets, and that was okay. You know why? Because I got up, got dressed, and worked harder to find out what I could accomplish.

My biggest obstacle was always me. I worried about what others would think of me, especially my family when this book was published. Fear slowed me down so many times it physically and mentally hurt to move forward. I was impatient and wanted answers immediately. I would push forward, because that's what I had learned from society—push until it gets done. I had forgotten about delayed gratification, like I experienced as a child. Nothing was instant in the 1970's—no instant TV, texts, or video games.

I spent time with my family and friends, playing in the woods. I was connected in my youth and lost some of that connection as I grew older. I had to learn to relax and be patient. The answers I asked for would always be given. All I needed to do was pay attention to receive. In order to pay attention, I had to learn how to quiet my very chatty mind through meditation. Sitting in a quiet room didn't work for me, so I had to find another way. What did work was cleaning horse stalls. My body was busy, giving my mind time to relax and tune into my inner guidance.

I learned by observing and listening to people around me that many run on fear of not knowing what to do when an unpleasant situation arises. Our inner guidance and the natural world hold all the answers. It just requires quieting the mind and having patience, trust, belief, gratitude, inner guidance, and most importantly, respect.

The good news is all of these fears can be overcome with work, perseverance, and a willingness to believe and accept the natural world we live with every day of our lives. Nature truly is healing and nurturing when we take the time to build a relationship with her. Earth is an amazing being when her rhythms and patterns are experienced, as those very same patterns and rhythms lie within our hearts as well. I found the answers I was looking for and you can too. The answers are right in front of us; they always have been and always will be.

I have experienced a world of energy, one that must be highly respected and worked with in a state of love. That being said, I believe energy exists in many forms, in many planes of existence, and within us. Don't take my word for it; seek out your own truths and answers. Always be guided by your heart, intuition, or gut instinct, whatever label you want to attach to it. If something feels wrong or off to you, honor that feeling and listen to it. I did not honor my intuition the night I hurt Chloe, and that was a painful lesson to learn. I have also come to the conclusion that energetic table healing is not my calling. Most importantly, seek out trusted advisors to help you on your journey. Question everything you see, feel, and experience. Build and establish a support group of like-minded people with positive attitudes.

I have learned to create a world of inner peace while life around me explodes in chaos. I choose to be in a state of positive thought and away from drama, for drama creates chaos.

I would like to share this story with you. One day I went to pick Rebecca up from work. As I pulled into the parking lot, I drove my car toward a section that faced the highway. Turning off the ignition, I relaxed and began to stare at the cars speeding by, my mind slipping away into its quiet place. A few minutes later I had a revelation. I was watching the reality of each individual driver, and their combined reality blended into my own. I wondered, could that really be? Are we really the sum total of each other's reality playing out as one consciousness? Did we really have control over that consciousness? I have found the answer I needed; now it's time to find your own.

There is a huge shift in the collective consciousness of the world, a time of reflection of the choices that have taken us to where we are in our lives. A choice to sit and suffer in the pain and hardship we have created for ourselves or to move forward and live a different way. You and I, the collective whole, can change our lives and the world around us.

On June 1, 2014, I sat alone on a bench at an inter-tribal powwow. Watching my daughter and her friends dance made me so proud of how far these young ladies have grown. Earlier in the day, Rebecca had reminded me it was indeed June 1. Three years to the day, the tornado had blasted into my life. I reflected not on the pain anymore but on how much I had grown in those three years. A beautiful acknowledgment came from the very thought floating through my mind. A yellow and black butterfly flew past me and I smiled, for I knew my transformation had been completed for this book. My heart had grown and I had changed. I became an author. Another door had been opened for the next book, a historical fiction.

I wondered how I could end this book, but how can I end something that is infinite? I can't. My growth is an ongoing process, and my journey will continue long after I leave the physical plane. Therefore, I am living my life on my terms with guidance purer than logic, my heart and Spirit. You can do the same. I feel it.

Reference Materials

Below is a list of business professionals who have assisted in the front cover design or in some aspect of my journey of transformation and growth. For more information please visit my site.

Jen Barlow
www.jenbarlow.com

Elizabeth Ellen Photography
www.elizabethellen.com

Mohawk Leathers; Craig and Eileen Standing Bear
www.MohawkLeathers.com
cestandingbear@verizon.net

Peaceful Hearts Certified Master Hypnotherapist
www.peacefulhearts.net
peacefulhearts@charter.net

Primary Concepts Advertising Design
www.primaryconceptsdesign.com
primaryconcepts1@verizon.net

Facebook Pages

Elizabeth Ellen Photography https://www.facebook.com/elizabethellen photography

Grandmother Tree Herbals https://www.facebook.com/pages/Grandmother-Tree-Herbals/173373832735909

Odyssey of the Spirit Shoppe-Official Designer of the Author's Experience Basket https://www.facebook.com/odysseyofthespirit

Peaceful Hearts: Healing through Hypnosis https://www.facebook.com/pages/Peaceful-Hearts-Healing-through-Hypnosis/215948425254867

Tehya Natane's Creations/ Custom Jewelry_https://www.facebook.com/pages/Tehya-Natanes-Creations/510167739118894.

Printed in the United States
By Bookmasters